The Mysterious  & Unknown

Pyramids

by Charles George

ReferencePoint Press™

San Diego, CA

For more information, contact
ReferencePoint Press, Inc.
PO Box 27779
San Diego, CA 92198
www.ReferencePointPress.com

Picture credits:
AP/Wide World Photos, 28, 32, 39, 52, 55, 58, 65, 71, 78, 88, 90
The British Museum, 24
Dreamstime, 30
Photos.com, 6, 10, 13, 16, 21, 26, 42, 46, 83
Steve Zmina, 14–15

Series design and book layout:
Amy Stirnkorb

LIBRARY OF CONGRESS CATALOGING-IN-PUBLICATION DATA

George, Charles, 1949-
 Pyramids / by Charles George.
    p. cm. -- (Mysterious and unknown)
 Includes bibliographical references and index.
 ISBN-13: 978-1-60152-027-2 (library)
 ISBN-10: 1-60152-027-1 (library)
 1. Pyramids--Miscellanea. I. Title.
 BF1999.G3383 2007
 909--dc22
                                                              2007010342

CONTENTS

FOREWORD

"Strange is our situation here upon earth."
—Albert Einstein

S ince the beginning of recorded history, people have been perplexed, fascinated, and even terrified by events that defy explanation. While science has demystified many of these events, such as volcanic eruptions and lunar eclipses, some continue to remain outside the scope of the provable. Do UFOs exist? Are people abducted by aliens? Can some people see into the future? These questions and many more continue to puzzle, intrigue, and confound despite the enormous advances of modern science and technology.

It is these questions, phenomena, and oddities that Reference-Point Press's *The Mysterious & Unknown* series is committed to exploring. Each volume examines historical and anecdotal evidence as well as the most recent theories surrounding the topic in debate. Fascinating primary source quotes from scientists, experts, and eyewitnesses, as well as in-depth sidebars further inform the text. Full-color illustrations and photos add to each book's visual appeal. Finally, source notes, a bibliography, and a thorough index provide further reference and research support. Whether for research or the curious reader, *The Mysterious & Unknown* series is certain to satisfy those fascinated by the unexplained.

INTRODUCTION

The excavation had taken 4 years—4 years of heat, humidity, and choking dust, 4 years of backbreaking work, digging deeper and deeper into the pyramid, 4 years of chipping away limestone, of hauling away rock and rubble, 4 years to clear a steep stone stairway and then a narrow corridor. But what lay at the end of the corridor?

At last, on July 15, 1952, deep within the pyramid of the Temple of Inscriptions, in the Mayan city of Palenque, a workman's crowbar broke through a wall of rubble at the end of the corridor. Shining a spotlight through the gap, Mexican archaeologist Alberto Ruz Lhuillier peered inside, glimpsing what no human had seen for more than 1,000 years. He later wrote about the experience:

> Out of the dim shadows emerged a vision from a fairy tale, a fantastic, ethereal sight from another world. . . . Delicate festoons of stalactites hung like tassels of a curtain, and the stalagmites on the floor looked like drippings from a great candle. The impression, in fact, was that of an abandoned

The tomb of Pacal the Great was discovered in 1952 in the Mayan city of Palenque.

chapel. Across the walls marched stucco figures in low relief. Then my eyes sought the floor. This was almost entirely filled with a great carved stone slab, in perfect condition.[1]

After clearing the entrance to the tomb, Ruz Lhuillier squeezed through:

> I entered the mysterious chamber with the strange sensation natural for the first one to tread the entrance steps in a thousand years. I tried to see

it all with the same vision that the Palenque priests had when they left the crypt; I wanted to . . . hear the vibrations of the last human voices beneath these massive vaults; . . . to capture the cryptic message that those men of old had given us. . . . Across the impenetrable veil of time I sought the impossible bond between their lives and ours.[2]

What he mistook for floor turned out to be a solid limestone slab 12 feet (3.7m) long and 7 feet (2m) across, weighing 5 tons (4.5t). Since its discovery, its delicately carved surface has come to be considered one of the most extraordinary examples of Mayan sculpture. Ruz Lhuillier believed the massive stone to be the lid of a sarcophagus, a stone coffin. After weeks of preparation, his workmen raised the slab with automobile jacks. Underneath, they found a second slab, with stone plugs at each end. Once they raised the upper slab high enough, Ruz Lhuillier climbed between the stones, removed one of the plugs, and peered inside: "My first impression was that of a mosaic of green, red, and white. Then it resolved itself into details—green jade ornaments, red painted teeth and bones, and fragments of a mask. I was gazing at the death face of him for whom all this stupendous work—the crypt, the sculpture, the stairway, the great pyramid with its crowning temple—had been built."[3] Ruz Lhuillier and his team had found the remains of one of the most powerful Mayan kings—Pacal the Great.

Before their discovery, few archaeologists believed Mayan pyramids were more than platforms for temples. No one imagined that some served as tombs, like the pyramids of Egypt. Even modern-day Maya knew little about the ruins, other than to

The floor of the
tomb of Pacal the
Great is considered
one of the most
extraordinary
examples of Mayan
sculpture.

avoid them after dark, fearing the spirits they believed inhabited them.

But the clues were there just waiting to be noticed. One section of the flagstone floor in the sanctuary atop the pyramid had small holes in it, with stone plugs filling each hole. Explorers and scientists had studied the architecture and hieroglyphs of this temple-topped pyramid since 1831. Scores of scholars and tourists had walked across this floor without stopping to wonder about the two rows of curiously plugged holes, but Ruz Lhuillier, intrigued by them, began digging to discover what they were, and the rest, as they say, is history.

All over the World

Around the world, on virtually every continent, ancient pyramids rise from deserts, fields, and jungles. Some are large, others small. Some served as tombs; others did not. Some are stone monuments, others adobe brick or packed earth. In most cases, scholars know who built them and when. In others, they cannot be sure. In almost every case, it is difficult to imagine how ancient peoples, without today's heavy equipment, managed to build such massive structures.

It is also hard to know precisely why these people built pyramids. Experts can speculate as to why and, in some cases, be reasonably sure they know the answers, but they can never be 100 percent sure. Theories abound, some firmly grounded in science, while others are based on wild conjecture. Because of that uncertainty, all pyramids share one thing in common. They are a never-ending source of mystery. And humans have always enjoyed a good mystery.

CHAPTER 1

The Pyramids of Giza

When people hear "pyramid," most think of Egypt, and in particular, the pyramids on the Giza Plateau, outside Cairo. There, between the lush Nile Valley and the endless sands of the Libyan Desert, stand massive pyramids built to honor three pharaohs—Khufu, Khafre, and Menkaure—who ruled Egypt during a period known as the Old Kingdom (ca. 2700-2200 BC).

No structures on earth are more recognizable or have been more carefully studied, yet many questions remain. Later pyramids in Egypt contain hieroglyphs explaining who, when, why, and in some cases, how they were built, but the Giza pyramids do not. Most scholars believe they know approximately when these pyramids were constructed and who ordered them built, but some skeptics disagree. Scholars also disagree about why they were built—whether intended as pharaohs' tombs or merely as monuments in their honor. Some speculate that the pyramids

Egypt's Giza Plateau contains the world's best known pyramids. The smallest of the three main pyramids, Menkaure's, is shown with its three lesser pyramids.

may have been constructed for other, as yet undiscovered, purposes.

The most common mysteries associated with the Giza pyramids concern methods used in their construction. Most who study pyramids wonder how a culture that supposedly did not have the wheel, pulleys, or iron tools could have built such gigantic structures. For centuries, researchers also thought that the Giza pyramids were built primarily with slave labor. Recent discoveries dispute that idea, suggesting instead a paid labor force. One by one, theories have been studied, and one by one, they have either been proved or disproved through archaeological discovery and scientific analysis. The mystery surrounding the pyramids of Giza endures, however, because some theories have neither been proved nor disproved. They continue to intrigue scientists.

One writer, discussing questions that have been posed for centuries about these pyramids, says they have always been surrounded with a "tangle of conflicting theories, fables, and wild speculations." He lists various theories about their uses:

> A religious writer of the 12th century considered them the Biblical granaries of Joseph, built to survive Egypt's Seven Lean Years. Medieval Arabs thought them storehouses for the wisdom and riches of a long-departed civilization. More recent theories have even described pyramids as lookout towers, landing pads for ancient astronauts, and geodetic markers used to resurvey the land after the Nile's floods.[4]

A local Egyptian folktale speaks of the pyramids being a guide to the stars and prophecies of the future. Arab superstitions describe ghosts wandering passageways, including one naked woman with rotten teeth who tries to seduce trespassers and drive them mad.

Theories and legends abound, but solid evidence is hard to come by. John Clooney, longtime director of the Brooklyn Museum's Egypt Collection, wrote about this frustrating lack of written records and hard evidence about the pyramids: "[The Giza

pyramids] are still bewildering. We've no original sources that explain how or why the pyramids were built. And there are only a few references to pyramids in any ancient Egyptian text at all. I think that's extraordinary. . . . In fact, if the pyramids were not physically present today, I might doubt they ever existed on so grand a scale."[5]

How Old Are They, Really?

According to most archaeologists, the oldest of the Giza pyramids—the Great Pyramid— was built for Khufu, the second king of Egypt's Fourth Dynasty, around 2500 BC The design and construction were overseen by Khufu's brother, Hemienu. Some dispute this, claiming the pyramid must have been built thousands of years earlier. At any rate, for at least 4,500 years, the Great Pyramid has fascinated humankind. But how long is 4,500 years? One writer, Daniel Loxton, puts the age of the pyramids into perspective by pointing out that, when Jesus Christ was born, the pyramids were already 2,500 years old:

> Imagine you have a time machine that can take you back in history in jumps of 100 years at a time. Now imagine that you are going to use your time machine to travel back to witness the construction of the Great Pyramid. One jump back, and the people you see ride in steam-powered trains and horse drawn carriages. Two jumps and they're in wooden sailing ships, while the first steam trains are just being invented. Three jumps—just 300 years—and Benjamin Franklin is a newborn infant. Six jumps and most Europeans don't know North America

even exists (or vice versa). In leaps of 100 years, you'd have to make 45 jumps to watch the construction of the Great Pyramid. (Maybe more.)[6]

Generations have come and gone, and yet the Giza pyramids are still there, and the Great Pyramid is the only structure listed as one of the Seven Wonders of the Ancient World that still stands. All others have been destroyed, either by nature or by man. The pyramid, despite being the oldest structure on that list, is relatively intact after 45 centuries of neglect, wars, earthquakes, tourists, sandstorms, and tomb robbers. As one Arab proverb puts it, "All things dread Time, but Time dreads the Pyramids."[7]

The pyramid of Khafre, seen here, was built during a period known as the Old Kingdom (ca. 2700–2200 BC).

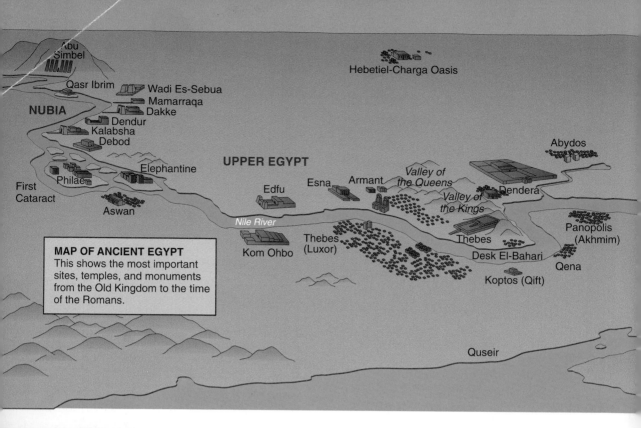

MAP OF ANCIENT EGYPT
This shows the most important sites, temples, and monuments from the Old Kingdom to the time of the Romans.

Abu Simbel

Qasr Ibrim

Wadi Es-Sebua
Mamarraqa
Dakke
Dendur
Kalabsha
Debod

NUBIA

Elephantine

Philae

First Cataract

Aswan

Hebetiel-Charga Oasis

UPPER EGYPT

Edfu

Esna

Armant

Valley of the Queens

Valley of the Kings

Dendera

Abydos

Panopolis (Akhmim)

Nile River

Kom Ohbo

Thebes (Luxor)

Thebes

Desk El-Bahari

Qena

Koptos (Qift)

Quseir

Preparing the Site for the Great Pyramid

Of all the pyramids in Egypt, none is more mysterious than the Great Pyramid. Unfortunately for Egyptologists, Khufu left no written account of how it was built. Without hieroglyphic evidence, scholars must theorize about methods used to level the area, align the structure with true north, quarry the stones, and put them into place. All they have is the pyramid itself, a few artifacts unearthed nearby that date from the time of its construction, and paintings and ancient papyrus records from later dynasties that refer to Egyptian construction practices.

Khufu's designers and builders must have been gifted mathematicians, astronomers, architects, and engineers, because the precision they achieved is astounding. The land upon which the Great Pyramid stands is almost perfectly level. Today's builders have laser transits, GPS locators, and bulldozers

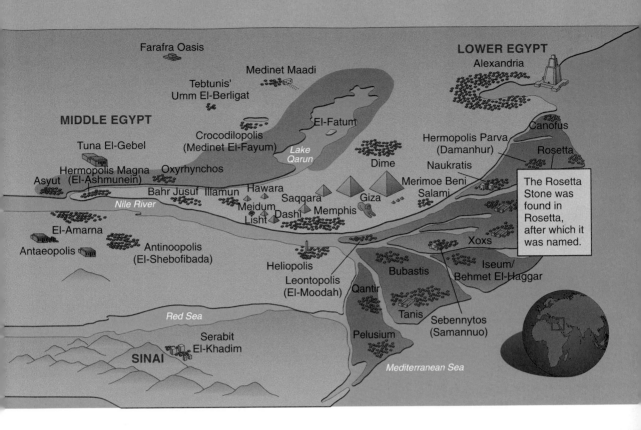

with which to measure and level a piece of ground. In ancient Egypt, scientists believe the pyramid's builders first dug a trench around the perimeter of the area and filled it with water. Knowing that water seeks its own level, they used the surface of the water to determine exactly how much soil to remove to level the area. There is evidence of such a trench on the Giza Plateau.

Once level was determined, workers performed the leveling with hand tools and manual labor. Precise leveling was essential for the stability of the structure. Even though the Great Pyramid covers 13.1 acres (5.3ha), the surface on which it stands varies less than 1 inch (2.5cm) in height across the entire area.

A Marvel of Precise Engineering

The Great Pyramid's 4 sides also demonstrate its builders' remarkable accuracy. The sides of its base form an almost perfect

The Great Pyramid, right, is nearly 490 feet tall and all four sides align almost perfectly with the cardinal directions, north, south, east and west.

square, varying less than 0.088 of 1 percent, despite the structure's immense size—756 feet (230m) per side. A pyramid's shape poses significant challenges, according to Dr. Gerhard Haeny, director of the Cairo-based Swiss Institute for Architectural and Archaeological Research. He explains that a cube, no matter its size, is relatively easy to build, but that a pyramid's:

> four sides slope smoothly up to a point—which, when you start, is only an imaginary one hundreds of feet above the desert. You can't sight on that point to check your work as you go up, because it doesn't exist. But if one face of your pyramid is just a little too steep, it will overshoot the others. . . . So once you lay the first course of stones, you're locked in.[8]

Since the Great Pyramid was nearly 490 feet (149m) tall, ancient Egyptian engineers' ability correctly to angle the sides to meet at the imaginary point at its apex becomes even more impressive.

Along with the pyramid's physical precision, its four sides almost perfectly align with the four cardinal directions—north, south, east, and west. Ancient astronomers knew by observation that stars seem to revolve around a certain point in the northern sky. They therefore considered that region of the night sky sacred, because its stars were visible throughout the night. It was considered indestructible, associated with the gods and eternity. Entrances to all Egyptian tombs face north for this reason, to help the deceased's soul ascend to the heavens. Some scientists believe the pyramid's designers determined true north by observing two particular stars' rotation around that sacred point and by aligning them with a plumb line when those stars were vertical.

This precise astronomical alignment is also apparent inside the Great Pyramid. According to astronomers, two narrow shafts leading outward from the king's chamber in the pyramid's center would have aligned precisely in 2500 BC with stars in Orion's belt and with the star Thuban, in the constellation Draco. These stars had special significance to the Egyptians. Orion was associated with the Egyptian god Osiris, and Thuban, at the time of the pyramid's construction, was the closest thing to a pole star in the northern night sky. The shafts were first thought to be air shafts, to help maintain a constant temperature inside the pyramid. Then, they were thought to be passageways leading to other hidden chambers. Small robots equipped with video cameras examined the shafts but found no such chambers.

Early Tourists

The pyramids of Giza were over 1,000 years old when Ramses II, ruler of Egypt from 1304 to 1237 BC, visited these ruins to offer his respects to his predecessors. Throughout the period in Egypt called the New Kingdom (1550–1070 BC), Egyptians came to Giza to view what they already considered ancient wonders. Some left graffiti scratched onto the stone surfaces, identifying themselves or perhaps asking the gods to favor them. Tourists from ancient Greece and from the Roman Empire also visited the pyramids of Giza.

Europeans as far back as the Renaissance have come to Cairo to see these wonders, many taking away souvenirs, as tourists do today. Some, hearing of passageways inside the Great Pyramid, insisted on stripping off most of their clothing and crawling through the narrow, bat-infested passages. Occasionally, one fainted from the heat, or perhaps from fear, and had to be removed like a cork from a bottle.

Builders of Man-Made Mountains

For centuries, one of the most perplexing mysteries associated with the Great Pyramid has been its actual construction. Who performed the physical labor? How did they transport and place the more than 2 million stones estimated to be in the pyramid, at an average weight of 3 tons (2.7t)? Khufu's pyramid, according to experts, was built within his 23-year reign. That would mean one stone would have been put into place every 2 minutes, assuming a workforce of around 30,000 to 40,000, working 10-hour shifts every day of the year.

Were these laborers slaves, as Greek historian Herodotus claimed in the fifth century BC? While visiting the pyramids, he talked with locals and later wrote that 100,000 slaves worked 30 years on the project. The pyramids were as ancient to him in the fifth century, however, as he is to us today. In addition, he was not always a reliable historian.

In fact, recent excavations near the Giza pyramids have uncovered the city that housed the workforce that built them, and most scientists now agree that Egyptian peasants, perhaps conscripted for the task, worked on the pyramids. Many were farmers whose fields flooded each year when the Nile rose from its banks, making farming impossible for a time. Near the pyramids, archaeologists Mark Lehner and Zahi Hawass have discovered the remains of mud-brick buildings—sleeping quarters, workshops, bakeries, breweries, and meetinghouses—and a workers' cemetery.

Corpses found at the cemetery indicate people who worked on the pyramids were relatively well fed and received medical attention. There is evidence, even in graves of common laborers, of individuals who received treatment for injuries and who survived for some time following those injuries. Some show signs of surgery. Estimates of the number of laborers needed to complete the pyramids now range from 15,000 to well over 100,000.

How the workers actually accomplished this monumental task is still a matter of speculation. Most archaeologists agree that the limestone blocks used in the structure were quarried nearby on the Giza Plateau. Masons worked the stone with copper chisels and stone hammers because they had no knowledge of iron. Once stones were cut and shaped, they were dragged to the pyramid, probably on wooden skids. Some stones, however, came from quarries farther away. These blocks, such as the red granite used to line burial chambers, were probably transported by barge along the Nile before being dragged to the pyramid along raised causeways.

Raising the Stones

How work crews got stones up onto the pyramid and into place is another mystery. Some believe they built a long, earthen ramp upon which to drag the stones. Due to the height of the final monument, though, this massive ramp would have extended far from the pyramid's base. Most scholars agree there would not have been enough room for such a ramp, had it extended all the way to the top levels of the pyramid, and that the amount of material needed for such a ramp would have doubled the amount of work needed to complete the project.

Another theory proposed a system of earthen ramps spiraling up the outside perimeter of the pyramid. Critics of this theory say it would have been difficult to secure this type of ramp to the pyramid's sloping sides. They also suggest that such ramps would have covered too much of the existing structure, making it virtually impossible for builders accurately to align the upper levels with those beneath the ramps.

Some researchers do not believe pyramids were used exclusively as burial places as some were discovered without coffins. This coffin, found in an Egyptian pyramid, indicates this pyramid was intended for burial purposes.

Did You Know?

Estimates of the number of laborers needed to complete the pyramids now range from 15,000 to well over 100,000.

By whatever route the stones were transported, they were quite heavy and would have required strong backs to move them. To make that job easier, work crews must have lubricated the ramps. Some Egyptologists believe they used a crude form of petroleum. Others believe vegetable oil more likely. Most think simply wetting the clay-rich soil of the ramps would have made them slick enough to ease the workers' burdens.

Were They Tombs, or Not?

However construction was accomplished, one of Egypt's most intriguing mysteries involves the purpose of the pyramids. Most Egyptologists believe they were built as tombs for pharaohs. Hieroglyphs allude to that fact. Other written sources also indicate this was the case. However, no pyramid has been found in modern times with an intact burial. Many pyramids contain stone sarcophagi dating to the time of their construction, and this strongly suggests the builders' intentions to bury someone inside. However, the burial chambers of many pyramids remained incomplete, never containing a sarcophagus. This has led some to question whether they were ever really intended as tombs.

Most scholars believe the function of pyramids as tombs becomes clearer when their gradual development from simple burial mounds to towering stone monuments is studied. Likewise, an understanding of Egyptian religion helps explain why this particular shape was chosen to house the mummified remains of Egyptian kings, and why the interiors of pyramid tombs were constructed, decorated, and furnished as they were. Finally, a logical explanation for the lack of intact pyramid burials may be that they were prominent landmarks and therefore obvious places to search for treasure. Perhaps their very existence inadvertently led to this enduring mystery.

CHAPTER 2

Houses of Eternity

Egyptian pyramids have been called resurrection machines, homes for the dead, stairways to heaven, vehicles to immortality, mounds of creation, and houses of eternity. Each hints at the primary use of pyramids and alludes to the central concept of Egyptian religion—a belief in an earthlike afterlife. This belief also reflects how Egyptians prepared their dead and their burial chambers.

Egyptian Religious Beliefs

Egyptian belief in an afterlife began during prehistory. Each year at about the same time, the Nile flooded, bringing nutrient-rich silt to the Nile Valley. Once floodwaters receded, crops flourished, providing bountiful harvests. The regular cycle of death and rebirth that Egyptians observed in nature, and the abundance they believed their gods provided each year, led residents of the Nile

Valley to view those gods as mostly benevolent. They considered their lives blessed and, as a result, did not fear death as much as many other ancient cultures did. This influenced their concept of the afterlife. They saw it as an opportunity to enjoy the pleasures of this world throughout eternity and therefore equipped their tombs with everything they would need for such a long period.

Early Egyptians covered their graves with mounds of earth topped with stones. Later Egyptians built more complex burial structures, first of mud brick, then of stone. All symbolized what they believed existed at the creation of the world. According to their mythology, in the beginning was darkness. Then a vast, formless ocean called Nu appeared. Out of this ocean a great mound arose, and from the mound came Ra (sometimes spelled Re), the sun god. Egyptians believed he created the earth and sky and that his tears fell to earth and became the first men and women.

Egyptians believed the sun god, Ra, created the earth and sky and that his tears became the first people on earth.

Egyptians believed that those first people, and the generations that followed them, were more than physical bodies. Egyptians believed each individual consisted of many elements, each requiring specific treatment at death. The physical elements included the body (called *sah)* and the heart (called *ib).* Egyptians believed *ib* was the seat of intelligence and emotion. Spiritual elements included *ka,* the life force or soul; *ba,* the personality or spirit; *akh,* an immortal joining of the *ka* and *ba; ren,* the individual's name; and *shuwt,* the person's shadow.

When the creator god Khnum molded every person from clay at

birth, he created a spiritual replica, the *ka*. After death, Egyptians believed the *ka* remained in the tomb and absorbed life-giving properties from offerings left by mourners. Usually, a statue of the deceased was included in the tomb for the *ka* to inhabit. The *ba*, or personality, was depicted as a human-headed bird that flitted about at will, yet always returned to the body, its perpetual roost. After a person's death, the *ba* traveled through the underworld, overcoming a series of trials, and then rejoined the *ka*, becoming the eternal and ideal form of existence—the *akh*.

Egyptians believed life after death could be enjoyed by the *akh* only if three conditions were met by the deceased's family. First, the person's body had to be well preserved, which required mummification. Second, the family had to provide sustenance, in the form of offerings. Finally, the person's name had to be commemorated through prayer. Each is reflected in Egyptian burials, from the simple pits of early Egypt to the elaborate pyramid tombs of later dynasties.

Early Burials

In ancient Egypt, before there were pharaohs, people lived in small towns and farming villages. They raised families, gathered crops, and harvested fish from the Nile. Near the river, all was well. Beyond the protection of the valley, however, lay unforgiving desert, where little could survive. Because of a lack of trees, people built houses out of mud brick or stone to shelter their families. Lumber was quite scarce. Mud and stone, though, were plentiful.

When people in ancient Egypt died, family members wanted to provide safe places for the bodies to rest, because they believed in an afterlife. They felt departed spirits would need their bodies on the other side. In death, as in life, shelter was necessary. But,

Many pyramids contain art that depicts everyday events the dead might expect in the afterlife.

again, wood was hard to find, so there were few wooden coffins. Instead, early Egyptians dug shallow pits, wrapped the dead in linen, and placed the body inside, with personal possessions and food offerings. Families then covered the grave with large stones to keep wild animals from digging up the body.

As Egyptian society progressed, people wanted larger, more ornate tombs, so their ancestors would be better equipped for the journey to the afterlife. This required more space for necessary items. Underground tombs, some with extensive passageways and outer chambers, were carved out of limestone bedrock. One-story buildings were constructed above them, with a vertical shaft joining this world with the dead's eternal home.

These rectangular mud-brick structures, with flat roofs and slightly sloping walls, are called mastabas, an Arabic word that means "benches." Some of the larger mastabas were 12 feet (3.7m) tall, with numerous chambers, including a chapel where the living came with daily offerings of food and drink for the deceased. In many cases, the interior walls of the mastaba were painted with murals depicting everyday events the deceased might expect in the afterlife. Mastabas continued as the preferred tomb among the middle classes of Egypt throughout the age of pyramids.

Mummification

Like Egypt's burial practices and rituals, mummification began rather simply and evolved into more complex ceremonies. It actually began as a natural process. Burying a body in desert sand created a "natural" mummy, dried and preserved by the arid conditions. Over time, Egyptians chose to enhance what nature accomplished in order to provide the dead with more perfectly preserved corpses. What evolved was a complex procedure that took several weeks.

First, embalmers washed and purified the body. All internal organs except the heart were removed, either through the body's various openings or through an incision in the abdomen. The heart was left in place because Egyptians believed it was the seat of all thought. All other organs were preserved in four vessels of wood, stone, or pottery called canopic jars. Embalmers removed the brain through the nose and discarded it. They believed it served no function.

Once the internal organs were removed, the corpse was washed and dried, scented, and filled with temporary packing and natron, a natural salt that dehydrated the tissues. Natron was also placed over the corpse's surface for 40 days. During this time, the body

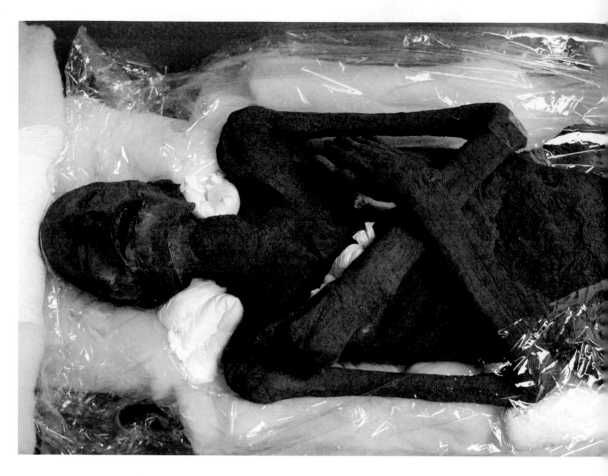

This mummy, found in Egypt in 2000, was DNA-tested and found to be that of Rameses I.

lost up to 75 percent of its weight. At the end of 40 days, embalmers removed the packing and inserted fresh natron and resin-soaked linen into the body cavity to restore its normal shape.

Finally, attendants coated the corpse in cedar oil and scented resins, wrapped it in linen bandages along with protective amulets and charms, and placed it in its coffin. During this part of the ritual, priests read aloud incantations from *The Book of the Dead*, a collection of prayers, magic spells, and hymns designed to guide and protect the dead on their journey through the underworld.

Pyramid Tombs

As Egyptian embalming techniques became more complex, so did their tombs. Around 2630 BC, a Third Dynasty pharaoh, Djoser, asked Imhotep, his vizier (chief counselor), to build his tomb at Saqqara, near the Egyptian capital of Memphis. Instead of a one-story mastaba, Imhotep designed a structure with progressively smaller mastabas, stacked one on top of another, thus creating the Step Pyramid—the world's first stone monumental building and the world's first pyramid. It stood at the center of a large, walled complex of structures including a ceremonial court and mortuary temple.

Djoser's burial chamber was carved into the limestone beneath the pyramid, amid a maze of passageways, treasure rooms, and burial chambers for him and family members. Imhotep apparently designed Djoser's inner tomb to mimic the pharaoh's palace. Outside, the Step Pyramid resembles a six-step stairway and, according to Egyptologists, was intended to symbolize a stairway to heaven, a vehicle from which Djoser's spirit could ascend, joining Egyptian gods in the sky.

Fifty years after Djoser's death, the pharaoh Snefru built 3 pyramids. The first, the Collapsed Pyramid, is at Meidum, 40 miles (64.4km) south of Memphis. It scarcely resembles a pyramid. On its northern face, a steeply descending passageway drops below bedrock and levels out for a short distance before rising again into an abandoned and unfinished burial chamber.

Snefru then commissioned 2 pyramids at Dahshûr, 5 miles (8km) south of Memphis. One is the Bent Pyramid, so called because its slope abruptly changes halfway up. Its burial chambers lay below ground level, carved into the limestone. It is the only pyramid with 2 entrances—one on the north, like most other pyra-

Djoser's Step Pyramid, seen here, is at Saqqara, near Memphis. It was built around 2630 BC.

mids, that leads to a subterranean chamber, and another on the west, that leads upward to a vault built within the pyramid itself. Scientists disagree as to the intended function of the upper chamber. Both chambers were empty when archaeologists first explored them in 1838.

Snefru's other pyramid, the Red Pyramid, is considered the world's first "true pyramid" because it has smooth, flat sides. Its north-facing entrance descends to two chambers lying side by side in the heart of the pyramid. The burial chamber was concealed above these twin rooms but contained no physical remains when first discovered by archaeologists. The Red Pyramid was originally 345 feet (105m) tall, the tallest structure in the world when it was built.

Snefru's son Khufu and Khufu's successors built pyramid tombs at Giza. Other, smaller pyramids were built nearby. Still others were built by later pharaohs in other parts of Egypt. In all, about 100 pyramids were constructed in Egypt and nearly 200 in Nubia, a kingdom to the south, in present-day Sudan. Each was different, but the basic design of their inner tombs was similar.

Deep within the heart of the pyramid lies the burial chamber, reached by often narrow, steep passageways. Outer rooms, built to hold household goods, furniture, clothing, food, statues, and sometimes boats or chariots, served to provide for the deceased in the afterlife and to distract tomb robbers from the actual burial chamber. False walls, secret doors, booby traps, and sometimes hieroglyphs warning of curses on those who disturbed the tombs were supposed to ensure the eternal rest of the deceased, but they did not always work.

Tomb Robbers

Pyramids are prominent, highly visible structures. They tower over the landscape, dwarfing everything else for miles. In ancient Egypt, everyone knew they contained unimaginable riches. They also knew there had to be an entrance. As a result, pyramids were easy targets for tomb robbers. One writer describes the discovery of the skeleton of one unlucky looter centuries after his entry into a tomb:

> [Tomb builders] employed everything from bolts to false passageways, sliding trapdoors of stone, and overhead shafts filled with rubble that came

A man stands on the Red Pyramid; in the background is the Bent Pyramid. The Red Pyramid is considered to be the first true pyramid.

crashing down on anyone trying to dig through such a barrier. Grisly evidence of at least one robber caught at his thievery showed up in a tomb. An archaeologist working there found a pair of severed arms atop a shattered coffin, with the victim's bones lying alongside. The scientist surmised that a robber had been about to lift the mummy from its casket when the tomb's ceiling collapsed, cutting off the arms and at the same time killing him.[9]

Apparently, tomb robbing was rampant in Egypt, even during the days of the pharaohs. One papyrus hieroglyphic court document records a tomb robber's confession:

> We went to rob the tombs in accordance with our regular habit and found the pyramid of King Sekemre-shedtawy. We took our copper tools and we broke into this pyramid through its innermost part. Then we broke through the rubble and found the pharaoh lying at the back of his burial place. The noble mummy was completely bedecked with gold, and his coffins were adorned with gold and silver inside and out and inlaid with all sorts of precious stones.[10]

Thieves took anything of value and set fire to coffins. This common practice freed whatever gold foil might still be clinging to the wood. What was left of the burned mummies was probably thrown out into the desert.

With so much buried treasure so widely known and with most having few guards, few tombs have escaped thieves, who have robbed almost every memorial in Egypt. At one point during the New Kingdom, Egyptian officials themselves broke into the few tombs that had not yet been looted, removed the mummies, labeled them for future identification, and hid them in secret places to protect them.

An Undisturbed Pyramid Tomb?

In 1951, Zakaria Goneim, of Egypt's Antiquities Department, discovered the buried foundation of a previously unknown

Texts
for the Dead

Beginning at the end of the Fifth Dynasty, inner walls of pyramid tombs featured hieroglyphs that explained much of what Egyptians believed about the afterlife. In the tomb of Unas, who ruled Egypt around 2490 BC, the walls are almost completely covered. Archaeologists believe the 759 different spells in the Pyramid Texts were once recited during mummification and burial ceremonies. Spell 303, for example, reflects beliefs that the deceased sails to heaven on a raft: "O you western, eastern, southern, and northern gods! The four purified reed-rafts which you laid down for Osiris when he came to the sky so that he could sail across the sky with his son Horus beside him, so that he could lift him up and make him appear as a great god in the sky—lay them down for me too!"

In later dynasties, burial texts were not inscribed on tomb walls but on the inner walls of coffins. These coffin texts reflected concerns about the ordeal a person's spirit would have to undergo on its way to the afterlife. Later, during the New Kingdom, the dead were buried with papyrus scrolls inserted within their linen bandages. These were called *The Book of Coming Out into the Day*, but Egyptologists call them *The Book of the Dead.* They contain about 200 spells designed to provide the deceased with magic to assist them through their trials. The most famous, Spell 125, advises the deceased on how to answer questions about his or her actions in life during judgment by Osiris: "I have told no lies, I have stolen no food, I have not done any wrong, I have witnessed no crime."

Quoted in Christine Hobson, *The World of the Pharaohs: A Complete Guide to Ancient Egypt.* New York: Thames and Hudson, 1987, pp. 168, 170.

pyramid at Saqqara. Its entrance was blocked with sand and rubble, leading Goneim to hope the tomb had not been looted. If so, he had found what no modern archaeologist had found before—an undisturbed, intact pyramid burial chamber.

Surely, robbers would not have bothered resealing the tomb after removing its treasure. When Goneim and his team entered the underground passageways, they found 132 storage chambers, many containing stone, alabaster, and clay vessels. The discovery of gold jewelry in one of the rooms caused their spirits to soar. Then, Goneim's team found the hidden entrance to the burial chamber. After removing the stone that sealed its entrance, they cautiously made their way inside. Goneim later described what he found:

> At last, when the final stone was removed, I crawled forward on my belly, electric torch [spotlight] in hand. We had broken through the blockage near the roof of a large vault. Below was black emptiness. Without further hesitation, I plunged, half-falling, half-scrambling, to the floor of the chamber. When we [Goneim and his assistant] had picked ourselves up and a lamp was raised, a wonderful sight greeted us. In the middle of a rough-cut chamber lay a magnificent sarcophagus of pale, golden, translucent alabaster. We moved towards it. My first thought was, "Is it intact?"[11]

Sure enough, it was untouched, still sealed with the original plaster and draped with decayed plant remains, perhaps a wreath left by mourners.

Goneim's team was ecstatic. Here at last was a pyramid that actually contained the physical remains of its pharaoh. After a month of careful preparations, they slowly raised the 500-pound lid (227kg) of the stone sarcophagus, and Goneim peeked inside. It was empty! In fact, the sarcophagus showed no evidence of having held a mummified pharaoh.

If it had never held a mummy, then why was it so carefully sealed? Why had a wreath been left? Why the hundreds of vessels? And why was the tomb sealed so carefully and so completely? What purpose had it served? Egyptologists cannot agree on answers.

Finding a pyramid sealed but empty is not unique. Even the Great Pyramid, when first unsealed by Arab caliph Abdullah al-Mam'ūn in the ninth century AD, was empty. When he and his crew finally removed the blocking stones from the inner passageways of the pyramid and reached the sepulcher, they found only a large, bare chamber with no hieroglyphs or markings of any kind, containing a lidless, empty, unmarked stone coffin. Despite centuries of disappointment, Egyptologists still hope a previously unknown pyramid will be discovered with an intact tomb. The search goes on.

Did You Know?

It was not uncommon for a tomb to be found intact, sealed, but empty.

CHAPTER 3

Pyramids of Mesoamerica

Pyramids in Egypt are famous. Those in Sudan are numerous. But nothing on the African continent can compete with the number and diversity of pyramids dotting the landscapes of the Americas. Mysteries surround American pyramids because of the large number of unexplored sites. Pyramids in Egypt have been studied for centuries, but the systematic study of American pyramids spans only 150 years.

Mesoamerica, which includes Mexico and Central America, was home to numerous civilizations with traits similar in some ways to Egypt—construction and use of stone pyramids and temples, hieroglyphic writing, a complex religion worshipping many gods, and a belief in life after death. However, they also possessed two traits unique to the region, and these were directly related to pyramids—religious ceremonies featuring ritual bloodletting or human sacrifice and a complex sacred calendar. Most prominent among

Mesoamerican civilizations were the Mayan and the Aztec, but they were not the first to build and use pyramids.

Mesoamerica's First True City—Teotihuacán

Around 200 BC, Mesoamerica's first city—Teotihuacán—was established in the Valley of Mexico, northeast of present–day Mexico City. Between AD 300 and 600, it had a population of between 75,000 and 200,000, making it the largest city in Mesoamerica and one of the largest in the world at that time. At its height, Teotihuacán contained 2,600 major structures, including step pyramids of various sizes. According to a 1962 aerial survey and mapping project, the carefully planned city covered more than 8 square miles (21 sq. km), making it larger than imperial Rome.

There are no written records of Teotihuacán's builders or people. Only a few symbols have survived, painted on walls or inscribed on pots, suggesting they may have had a written

At one time, the Teotihuacán, Mexico, site contained as many as 2,600 major structures and was one of the largest cities in the world.

language. Unfortunately, there are far too few examples to translate it. Neither do archaeologists know who built this great city or its original name. They call the city's inhabitants Teotihuacános. Many of the names associated with Teotihuacán came from the Aztecs, who arrived in the Valley of Mexico in the thirteenth century, long after this ancient city had been abandoned.

What the Aztecs discovered was a silent, crumbling ruin, but they were wonderstruck by the scope and artistry of the massive pyramids and wide boulevards of the haunting metropolis. They thought the city must have been built by gods. Aztecs regularly made religious pilgrimages to the city and called it Teotihuacán, or City of the Gods (sometimes translated Place Where Men Become Gods, or Place Where the Gods Were Conceived). They also named the city's most prominent landmarks the Pyramid of Tonatiuh (the Sun), the Pyramid of Metztli (the Moon), and, Miccaohtli, Avenue of the Dead. Another landmark, the Pyramid of Quetzalcoatl, the Feathered Serpent, sits in a large, enclosed plaza down the Avenue of the Dead from the two main pyramids. Spanish conquistadores called this plaza La Ciudadela, the Citadel.

Few tombs have been found in Teotihuacán. Scientists have uncovered ceremonial burials, but most of those bodies were sacrificial victims. Archaeologists, analyzing residential structures in the city, believe Teotihuacanos cremated their dead, wrapped the ashes in cloth, and buried them under the floors of their homes. This practice, which left no bones to examine, and the lack of a written language make learning about the Teotihuacanos more difficult, adding to the city's mystery. Despite these obstacles, archaeologists are gradually piecing together an image of the Teotihuacanos.

Pyramid of the Sun

The most striking monument in Teotihuacán is the massive Pyramid of the Sun. Visible for miles, this man-made mountain dominates the area. Built in 2 stages, beginning about AD 100, the pyramid is 738 feet (225m) on each side, and its base covers about 10 acres (4ha), almost exactly the same size as the base of the Great Pyramid. At 246 feet (75m) tall, it is less than half as tall as the Great Pyramid but still the tallest in Mesoamerica.

Exploratory tunnels dug in 1919 and 1932 found no burial chambers inside the Pyramid of the Sun, no secret passageways, no mummies, and no treasure. Instead, archaeologists discovered that, based on observed construction techniques, Teotihuacanos had a sophisticated understanding of engineering principles. Most of the interior of the pyramid consists of compacted mud reinforced with wooden poles. This technique apparently counteracted the natural outward push of the material, more or less maintaining the pyramid's shape for over 2,000 years.

In AD 400, when Teotihuacán was at its height, the pyramid had a flat-topped temple rising from its peak and was covered in thick plaster and painted an earthy red. Some evidence indicates its sides may have been decorated with brilliantly colored murals. Although scholars still refer to it as the Pyramid of the Sun, they do not know if it was built to honor the sun god. Only traces of the temple that stood atop the pyramid have survived, leaving archaeologists few clues about the pyramid's purpose. Some scholars believe it was built for the worship of Tlaloc, the god of rain.

In 1971, Mexican archaeologist Jorge Acosta made a startling discovery. He noticed that heavy rain had caused a depression at the foot of the Pyramid of the Sun. He dug there, finding the remains of a stairway that descended to a tunnel. The tunnel led to

The Pyramid of the Sun at Teotihuacán is the most striking monument in the site and is visible for miles.

a cave that extended far beneath the pyramid. At the end of the cave, directly beneath the center of the pyramid, scientists found a cloverleaf-shaped area, in which ceremonies apparently were performed. They found charcoal, suggesting ritual fires, and stone channels implying water rituals.

The cloverleaf shape of the end of the cavern suggests a connection to one of the oldest Mesoamerican myths—the Place of Emergence, a cave-womb from which the sun, the moon, and the founders of most Mesoamerican cultures emerged. The Aztecs called this cave Chicomoztoc, meaning Seven Caves. Mexican writer Jorge Pérez de Lara explains the significance of the cave to Mesoamerican mythology:

> The cave under the Pyramid of the Sun certainly contains many chambers, much in the man-

ner of the multi-lobed caverns often represented in Aztec codices, and brings to mind the story of . . . the mythical place of origin of the Aztec. From all indications, this myth must be very ancient. Throughout Mesoamerica, pyramids are regarded as symbolic mountains, while their temples are considered to be symbolic caves; mountains often are sacred places, while caves can be thought of not only as places of origin, but also as places of plenty.[12]

Since the Pyramid of the Sun was the first major structure built at Teotihuacán, scientists now believe the cave must have been especially sacred to the Teotihuacanos. They built the pyramid directly over it and built their city around it.

Recent Discoveries

At the southern end of the Avenue of the Dead lies the Pyramid of the Moon. Scientists knew it was built in stages over hundreds of years, but did not know what, if anything, was inside. Recently, to see if there was a royal tomb beneath it, Rubén Cabrera Castro, of Mexico's National Institute of Anthropology and History, and Saburo Sugiyama, of Japan's Aichi Prefectural University, tunneled deep inside the 140-foot-tall stone pyramid (43m). They discovered 5 bodies, but none was Teotihuacano royalty.

Instead, the common graves contained gruesomely disembodied heads and other remains of sacrificial victims, probably foreign warriors and dignitaries. Castro and Sugiyama also found animal remains. *National Geographic* writer A.R. Williams describes the intriguing discovery:

Evidence indicates that all the victims were ritually killed to consecrate successive stages of the pyramid's construction. The earliest sacrifice, from about AD 200, marked a substantial enlargement of the building. A wounded foreigner, most likely a prisoner of war, was apparently buried alive with his hands tied behind him. Animals representing mythical powers and military might surrounded him—pumas, a wolf, eagles, a falcon, an owl, and rattlesnakes—some buried alive in cages.[13]

The human victims were stripped of all ornamentation, beheaded, and thrown into a heap.

In an earlier excavation, Sugiyama discovered 133 skeletons with their hands tied inside the Pyramid of Quetzalcoatl. He also uncovered an abandoned tunnel leading to an empty, open pit deep within the pyramid. He wondered if there could have been a royal tomb there but found no physical proof.

Only 10 percent of Teotihuacán has been excavated. The remainder lies buried beneath farms, towns, highways, and a Mexican military base. Archaeologists are eager to learn more about the Teotihuacanos. Primarily, they want to know the meaning of the enigmatic symbols scattered through the city. Many are repeated and may have had special meaning, but no translation has been made so far.

The Maya

Teotihuacanos apparently had no written language, but the Maya were fully literate. Because Mayan hieroglyphs have been translated, scientists can read names, dates, and countless other details on stone pyramids in Mayan cities and ceremonial centers. This enables scientists to get a much clearer picture of Mayan society and history than is possible with other pre-Columbian civilizations. The Maya ruled a region that includes the present-day Mexican state of Chiapas, the Yucatán Peninsula, and the highlands of Guatemala, Honduras, Belize, and extreme western El Salvador. Their dominance lasted nearly 2,500 years, reaching its height in about AD 800. They created pyramids that rivaled those of ancient Egypt in size and artistry.

Archaeologists are able to say when most Mayan pyramids were built and by whom, thanks to hieroglyphic carvings on the structures. Unknown is how many other sites still lie undiscovered in the dense jungles of the Yucatán Peninsula and northern Central America. Dozens of Mayan centers have been found, each containing numerous pyramids. Some are in well-known ceremonial centers such as Tikal, Copán, Uxmal, Palenque, and Chichén Itzá. Others are in lesser-known, more recently discovered sites.

One such site, El Mirador, has not been excavated, and to the untrained eye, its structures look like tree-covered hills. At this site are a number of triadic structures, enormous, man-made platforms topped by 3 separate step pyramids. The 2 largest, nicknamed Pirámide del Tigre (Pyramid of the Tiger) and Pirámide de la Danta (Pyramid of the Tapir), reach a height of 183 feet (56m) and 236 feet (72m), respectively. When their excavation is complete, they may rival pyramids in better-known Mayan cities.

Did You Know?

Only about 10 percent of Teotihuacán has been excavated.

What Makes Mayan Pyramids Unique?

Mayan pyramids, in general, have three components: a stepped pyramidal base spanned by a stairway, a chambered sanctuary or temple atop the pyramid, and a purely ornamental masonry "top knot"—the roof comb—stretching skyward from the temple's roof. Though they serve no architectural purpose, these roof combs give Mayan pyramids their distinctive look. Tikal (which means "Place of Voices") has six large pyramids whose roof combs tower over the surrounding rain forest. Pyramids at Palenque, in the Mexican state of Chiapas, have evidence of roof combs, but theirs are different. Instead of the more solid combs of Tikal, each structure in Palenque is topped with a latticed roof comb, ornately carved with scenes from Mayan mythology. Another feature common to Mayan pyramids is found inside the sanctuaries. The Maya used corbeled arches in their construction. A corbeled arch is formed when stones on opposite walls are extended gradually toward the center of the open space until the opposite walls meet, forming a roughly triangular ceiling.

Two Mayan cities, Uxmal and Chichén Itzá, have pyramids that are unique in the Mayan world. At Uxmal, the Pyramid of the Magicians has an elliptical base, with rounded corners and rather steeply sloping sides. El Castillo, at Chichén Itzá, is an almost perfectly symmetrical square pyramid with stepped sides. It has a large temple at its peak with no roof comb, and stairways ascending the pyramid on all four sides.

Both pyramids have been fully excavated, revealing earlier pyramids underneath. Visitors at El Castillo enter an opening made by excavators, climb steps of an earlier pyramid to the temple at its top, and see the throne of Kukulcán, the Mayan equivalent of Quetzalcoatl, the Aztec feathered-serpent god.

New Guatemalan Highlands Discoveries

Though much about the Maya is already known, there are new discoveries being made almost daily, and each adds another piece to help solve the puzzle of this culture. Two such finds occurred recently, one by accident in 2001 and the other in 2005, at San Bartolo, just northeast of Tikal.

American archaeologist William Saturno was sent to San Bartolo to verify the existence of two stelae, ornately carved stone pillars. Not finding any at the site, and out of supplies, he ducked into a trench in the side of an unexcavated 85-foot pyramid (26m).

Cahokia and Its Mesoamerican Connection

Across the eastern United States, before the arrival of Europeans, archaeologists estimate there must have been hundreds of thousands of man-made earthen structures that resembled pyramids. Most were small burial mounds, but some were large earthen pyramids called temple mounds, built within cities occupied by people of the Mississippian culture. The largest of these Mississippian cities, Cahokia, located in East St. Louis, Illinois, contained over 100 flat-topped mounds and covered an area of 5 square miles (13 sq. km). At its

When he shone his flashlight into the gloom, he was amazed. He had stumbled upon one of the most important archaeological finds in the past several decades.

What he saw was the corner of an early Mayan mural—the face of the maize god looking over his shoulder at a beautiful maiden. The room was excavated, and the mural declared "the Sistine Chapel of the pre-Classic Maya world."[14] It depicts, in great detail, the Maya story of creation and the coronation of a king. According to Saturno:

height, between AD 1050 and 1250, as many as 10,000 people may have lived there.

Cahokia's central plaza featured 16 smaller flat-topped pyramids and an enormous earthen pyramid—Monk's Mound, the largest pre-Columbian earthwork in North America. This structure, said to have been built in stages over 300 years, today covers an area of 14 acres (5.7ha), larger than the base of Egypt's Great Pyramid. Monk's Mound measures 1,037 feet (316m) long, 790 feet (241m) wide, and 100 feet (31m) high. Some believe Cahokia's architecture reflects contact, most likely through trade, with early civilizations of Mesoamerica, probably Olmec or Mayan.

It was as if an ancient Maya book had been spread open before me, recounting the birth of the Maya cosmos from the gods' loins. . . . Clearly Maya painting had achieved glory centuries before the great works of the Classic Maya, in the 7th century. In Western terms, it was like knowing only modern art and then stumbling on a Michelangelo or a Leonardo [da Vinci]. . . . In short, this one chamber upended much of what we thought we knew about the early Maya.[15]

While Saturno and his team carefully worked on the mural beneath one San Bartolo pyramid, Guatemalan archaeologist Mónica Pellecer Alecio and her team were working at a smaller pyramid to the west. Finding signs of a sealed tomb and fearing looters, they excavated around the clock, finally uncovering what they believed to be the oldest known Mayan royal tomb. The skeleton they discovered wore a concave jade plaque, a symbol of Mayan royalty, and was buried with a vase bearing an effigy of Chac, the Mayan rain god. When the team removed the effigy, it began to rain, ending one of the region's worst dry seasons in a decade.

The Aztecs

Ancient cities have been lost before, but none fell so quickly or was so completely obliterated as the Aztec capital of Tenochtitlán. By 1523, less than four years after the arrival of Spanish conquistador Hernán Cortés, the Aztec capital had been destroyed. Despite being awed by Tenochtitlán and its monumental structures, Cortés was horrified by the Aztec practice of human sacrifice. His first orders were for the destruction of their main pyramid—Templo Mayor (Great Temple). A few generations later, after a colonial Spanish city had been built on the ruins of Tenochtitlán, the precise location of the ruins of Templo Mayor was a mystery. Some felt it was directly beneath the National Cathedral, symbolic of Christianity's defeat of paganism, but no one was sure.

However, in 1978, workers digging a ditch for an electric cable in the heart of Mexico City struck a large carved stone and immediately called for archaeologists. Beneath the street, they found a

large, round slab. Its carvings convinced scientists it must have stood at the foot of the Templo Mayor. Soon, the steps of the pyramid were found nearby, and since 1978, excavation has continued, gradually uncovering more and more of the lower portions of the structure. Leader of the dig, Mexican archaeologist Eduardo Matos Moctezuma, could scarcely believe how much of the original pyramid was still there.

Templo Mayor

Archaeologists uncovering the base of Templo Mayor discovered 86 offertory caches containing more than 6,000 objects. One stone-lined pit contained the skulls of 34 children, sacrificed to Tlaloc, the Aztec rain god. Excavators have also learned that the pyramid underwent 7 reconstructions during the 200 years of Aztec rule in the Valley of Mexico (AD 1325 to 1521), beginning with a simple mud-and-reed hut built in honor of Huitzilopochtli, the Aztec god of war and of the sun, when Tenochtitlán was founded. From that humble origin, the pyramid eventually reached a height of 197 feet (60m).

Hernán Cortés, writing to the king of Spain, could barely find words to describe the religious center of Tenochtitlán, site of the Templo Mayor:

> It is so large that in its precincts, which are surrounded by a wall, there could well lie a settlement of five hundred. Inside this area, about its edges, are fine buildings with large halls and corridors. There are at least forty pyramids, very tall and well made; the largest has fifty steps leading up to the main body of the pyramid. The principal pyramid

These re-mains of a young child, found in the Aztec ruins of the Templo Mayor in Mexico City, proved that the Aztecs sacrificed children.

is taller than the Seville [Spain] Cathedral's tower. The stone masonry and the woodwork are equally good; they could nowhere be bettered. All the stonework inside the temples where they keep the idols is sculptured, and the woodwork is all carved in relief and painted with pictures of monsters and other figures and designs.[16]

Before its destruction, Templo Mayor was a single pyramid, with twin staircases, topped by twin temples—one to Tlaloc and the other to Huitzilopochtli. Stepped pyramids were common in Mesoamerica, but the alteration of that form into a pyramid with two flights of stairs leading to double temples was unique to Aztec culture. Another structure unique to the Aztecs—the circular stepped pyramid dedicated to Ehecatl, the Aztec wind god—stood in front of Templo Mayor but has not yet been unearthed.

The World's Largest Pyramid

The world's largest pyramid lies southeast of Mexico City. The Great Pyramid of Cholula looks like a large hill from a distance but is actually a gigantic Aztec pyramid, the largest monument (by volume) ever built. Its sides measure 1,476 feet (450m), and it contains an estimated 5.8 million cubic yards (4.5 million cu. m) of stone and dirt, one-third larger than the Great Pyramid of Egypt.

A Spanish colonial church, Nuestra Señora de los Remedios (Our Lady of Remedies) was built atop the pyramid in 1594. Though archaeologists have tunneled extensively inside the Great Pyramid of Cholula, it may never be completely excavated or its mysteries revealed because of the presence of the historic church and nearby homes.

Did You Know?

The largest pyramid in the world is the Pyramid of Cholula, in Mexico City.

CHAPTER 4

Pyramids of South America

When most people think of pyramids in the Americas, they usually think of those in Mesoamerica. Few outside the field of archaeology have heard about pyramids in South America, even though many have been discovered along the western edge of the continent. Some are very old and some quite large. Mysteriously, the most familiar pre-Columbian culture in South America—the Inca—built few actual pyramids. Most South American pyramids predate the Inca Empire, some by millennia.

Many pre-Incan pyramids, called *huacas* by the Spanish, were constructed of adobe brick rather than stone, so their condition after centuries of erosion is not as good as that of stone pyramids. However, excavations at various pre-Incan sites have yielded surprising results. At least four pre-Incan cultures built pyramids as platforms for their temples and as tombs. Archaeologists are currently excavating in Peru—at Caral, a Norte Chico site north of

Lima; at several Moche sites near Trujillo and Chiclayo; and at the Nazca ceremonial center, Cahuachi. They are also excavating a large Tiwanaku pyramid called Akapana in the altiplano, or high plateau region, of northwestern Bolivia, near Lake Titicaca.

The Caral ruins in Peru are a vast complex that covers 165 acres.

Caral

Caral is a vast complex of pyramids, circular plazas, and other monumental architecture sprawling across 165 acres (67ha) in the arid plain above the Supe River Valley of Peru. The site was first discovered by American archaeologist Paul Kosok in 1948 but received little attention until recently. Peruvian archaeologist Ruth Shady Solís, who has been excavating Caral since 1994, believes it to be the oldest city in the Western Hemisphere, claiming it was inhabited from about 3000 to 1600 BC. Since the large city of Caral is surrounded by numerous other sites, as old but much smaller, she theorizes it was the capital of a civilization scientists call Norte Chico.

The Norte Chico employed a rather creative technique to construct monuments, and it was the analysis of this method that helped prove Shady Solís's dramatic claim. Determining the age of an archaeological site often requires radiocarbon dating, which requires organic matter such as grass, wood, or charcoal. The material tested from Caral was grass used in the construction of the pyramids. Roger Atwood, a contributing editor for *Archaeology* magazine, describes how grass came to be in the pyramids:

> To erect their structures, they [the builders of Caral] perfected the "shicra-bag" technique, by which armies of workers would gather a long, durable grass known as shicra in the highlands above the city, tie the grass strands into loosely meshed bags, fill the bags with boulders, and then pack the trenches behind each successive retaining wall of the step pyramids with the stone-filled bags. With bags acting as landfill, anchoring and reinforcing the structure at each stage, the people of Caral were able to build pyramids up to 70 feet tall.[17]

Shicra fibers are ideal for carbon testing because the grass dies after one season. With wood or charcoal, the carbon dating is less accurate because the tree it came from may have lived for centuries. With a grass that lives only one year, the dating is much more precise.

The results verified Shady Solís's suspicions about Caral and the surrounding villages. The Caral samples dated to 2627 B.C., and samples from a smaller pyramid site, Áspero, 20 miles (32km) away, dated to 3022 B.C. That means these sites were built some 4,700 years ago, at about the same time as the pyramids of Egypt. Evidence also suggests Caral was occupied for more than 1,000 years before being mysteriously abandoned.

One pyramid at Caral, Pirámide Mayor (Great Pyramid), covers an area the size of 4 football fields and is nearly 60 feet (18m) tall. Atop another pyramid, Pirámide de la Huanca (Pyramid of the Monolith), Shady Solis's team has uncovered the remains of a ceremonial hall with benches around a central fireplace. Artifacts uncovered at Caral include knotted strings similar to the Incan quipu (knotted strings with which the Inca kept records) and flutes made of condor and pelican bones. No traces of warfare have been found—no weapons, fortifications, militaristic art, or sacrificed bodies—leading scientists to infer that the city's builders were peace-loving, with a society founded on commerce and pleasure.

There is still much to be learned about Caral. Who were these people? Where did they come from? Archaeologists want to know what happened to the people they believe inhabited this city. Did their culture vanish completely, or did they merge with later cultures? Scholars want to see if this discovery will overturn long-held theories about how the Americas were populated, and when. If the Norte Chico people were already constructing complex cities with pyramids nearly 5,000 years ago along the western coast of South America, is it still logical to accept the theory that primitive humans first migrated from northeastern Asia to the Americas via the Bering Strait only 10,000 to 15,000 years ago? Or did the

Peruvian archaeologist Ruth Shady Solís believes Caral to be the oldest city in the Western Hemisphere, claiming it was inhabited from about 3000 to 1600 BC. The remains of this circular plaza sat in front of the main pyramid's base.

ancestors of those who built Caral arrive by boat from somewhere else? And, how did they influence later cultures, like the Moche?

The Moche Culture

The Moche civilization (sometimes called Mochica) flourished in what is now northern Peru from around the time of the birth of

Christ until about AD 800. They apparently did not have a written language, so most of what is known about them comes from their monumental structures (including enormous pyramids), elaborate pottery, and a few tombs discovered intact. The Moche also created a vast irrigation system to raise food in one of the most arid regions of the world. Faced with almost no rainfall, they harnessed runoff from the Andes to irrigate thousands of acres of arid land, producing abundant crops of corn, squash, beans, and peanuts.

One of the most prominent Moche structures is Huaca del Sol (Pyramid of the Sun), at a site believed to have been the capital and named for the Moche culture, near Trujillo, Peru. This massive pyramid was the largest solid adobe structure in the New World. Today, it stands more than 130 feet (40m) tall, but centuries of looting and erosion have reduced its original size. What remains of Huaca del Sol is perhaps only one-third as large as it once was, and it may have contained as many as 100 million adobe bricks. Scientists believe it was originally 164 feet (50m) tall, 1,150 feet (351m) long, and 538 feet (164m) wide. It is believed to have been used as a platform for religious rituals, a home for priests, and for burials.

Scientists are certain the Moche believed in an afterlife. As early as 1899, German archaeologist Max Uhle began uncovering Moche graves. He excavated 31 that lay between Huaca del Sol and Huaca de la Luna (Pyramid of the Moon), a smaller nearby pyramid. Each grave contained artifacts that suggest members of lower classes received ritual burials. In burials of every class, corpses have been found clutching sacred objects. Also, other worldly goods were buried with them, indicating the Moche believed they would need these objects in the afterlife.

But what about the pyramids themselves? Do they contain tombs? The Moche built hundreds of massive adobe step pyramids that intrigue archaeologists. Scientists wonder whether or not royal tombs were hidden within the pyramids and whether they contain treasure. The chances seem slim, however, because from the days of the Spanish conquest, *huaqueros*, or tomb robbers, have riddled the adobe pyramids with tunnels. Also during the Conquest, the Spanish redirected water from the Moche River, washing away a large portion of Huaca del Sol, looking for treasure.

Recent Moche Discoveries

In 1987, Peruvian archaeologist Walter Alva found the intact tomb of a Moche warrior-priest who ruled around AD 200. The tomb is located east of the Peruvian coastal city of Chiclayo, at an archaeological site known as Huaca Rajada (Opened Pyramid, or Broken Pyramid). The tomb had not been disturbed by looters. It contained a mummy and layers of treasure. The Lord of Sipán, as he was called, wore a solid gold headdress and pure silver sandals, along with numerous necklaces of copper, silver, and gold—one with beads in the shape of peanuts. Because of the tomb's riches, archaeologists have compared this find to that of the tomb of Tutankhamen in Egypt.

At both Huaca del Sol and Huaca de la Luna, and at another adobe pyramid at Moche, Huaca Cao Viejo (Pyramid of the Old Condor), scientists discovered evidence of a particularly brutal form of human sacrifice. Victims apparently were paraded naked and bleeding past a mural depicting earlier sacrificial victims marching to their doom. After seeing these images, victims were marched into a football field-size ceremonial plaza at the foot of the pyramid, where a

Moche priest slit each one's throat. A Moche priestess caught their blood in a goblet, which was given to a priest to drink.

Excavations at Huaca de la Luna in 1995 revealed the bones of more than 70 sacrificial victims. Some had their throats slit, some were beheaded, some were dismembered, and some had their skulls crushed. A nearby tomb contained a large wooden club stained with human blood. A later excavation found nine skeletons that appeared to have been butchered—the flesh removed from their bones.

Another tomb, believed to have been undisturbed since AD 450, was discovered in 2005 near the top of Huaca Cao Viejo. It contained the mummified body of a heavily tattooed Moche noblewoman. Her carefully prepared tomb contained a rich collection of funerary objects, including embroidered cloth, weaving tools, sheets of gold, and a gold-copper alloy. Oddly enough, her tomb also contained numerous weapons, including war clubs and spears. In a society archaeologists previously believed to have been entirely dominated by men, was this woman a ruler?

Everything uncovered at Moche sites in Peru suggests it was a rigid, authoritarian culture that waged war on neighbors. Because of ample crops provided by irrigation, and the bounty of the Pacific Ocean, the Moche prospered. Their leaders, warrior-priests, saw themselves as intermediaries between the living and the spiritual worlds. Because of its rigidity, the society was probably ill-equipped to handle natural catastrophes, which probably caused their sudden demise around AD 800.

Scientists now believe the Moche's end was caused by weather. They believe El Niño in the Pacific Ocean brought droughts, then disastrous floods to the area. El Niño is a south-flowing countercurrent in the Pacific Ocean that appears irregularly off the Peruvian coast, causing drastic changes in Western Hemisphere

Thor Heyerdahl

Thor Heyerdahl (1914-2002) was a Norwegian scientist who gained fame in 1947 by testing his theory that ancient peoples could have sailed across oceans to colonize other lands. To prove it, he and a team of adventurers built and sailed a balsa-wood raft from Lima, Peru, to Tahiti. They called it *Kon-Tiki* (another name for Viracocha, the Andean sun god adopted by the Inca). The 101-day, 4,300-mile voyage (7,000km) was a success. In 1970, he led another voyage, this time sailing a papyrus reed boat from western Africa to Barbados, in the West Indies.

In addition to his voyages, Heyerdahl led two archaeological excavations, one off the coast of Africa and another in Peru. In Tenerife, in the Canary Islands, Heyerdahl led a team excavating and restoring six mysterious stone step pyramids, the Pyramids of Güímar, that resemble Aztec pyramids. No one knows who built them, when, or why. Between 1988 and 1994, Heyerdahl also led excavations at Túcume, a pre-Incan site in northern Peru. Among the 26 pyramid-like adobe structures at Túcume, Heyerdahl found carved images of seagoing reed boats similar to the one he had used to cross the Atlantic.

weather patterns. Scientists believe this periodic climate change may have wreaked similar disasters on other cultures along the western coast of South America, including Cahuachi, capital city of the Nazca.

City of the Nazca

Farther south along the coast of Peru, etched into the surface of the barren Nazca Desert, lie hundreds of straight lines, geometric shapes, and images of animals and birds—figures known as the Nazca (or Nasca) Lines. These enormous etchings, called geoglyphs, were mysteriously created centuries ago and can be fully appreciated only when seen from the air. Scientists have long advanced theories about their purpose, but none has been proven.

South of the lines, archaeologists discovered what may solve this great puzzle—the remains of a vast ancient city with numerous pyramids. The largest ceremonial center in the world, the city covers nearly 10 square miles (26 sq. km). They now believe this city, called Cahuachi, is where the idea for the geoglyphs was conceived. Its excavation could provide answers about the people who created the Nazca Lines.

Although excavations began in the 1950s, no extensive studies were done until decades later. When Italian archaeologist Giuseppe Orefici arrived in 1983, Cahuachi resembled a range of low-lying hills. After years of excavation and study, the center is revealing itself. It is composed of 36 pyramids ranging in height from 49 feet (15m) to 115 feet (35m). Unlike most pre-Columbian ceremonial centers, Cahuachi (which means "from where you look" in Quechua, a South American Indian dialect) has no homes. Apparently, the center was used exclusively for religious ceremonies and burials, with only a few priests living there. Peruvian historian Josue

Lancho Rojas, Peru's leading expert on Nazca culture, has referred to Cahuachi as "the pre-Hispanic Vatican of its time."[18]

The primary structure in Cahuachi is a 7-level step pyramid called the Grand Pyramid or the Great Temple. It measures 92 feet (28m) tall, 361 feet (110m) long, and 328 feet (100m) wide and features adobe walls and geometric ramps. It was apparently constructed on a natural rise. Extensive plazas and terraces once covered the city, which may have been built as early as 100 BC.

Cahuachi is one of the most looted archaeological sites in the world. Thousands of Nazca graves have been destroyed by thieves looking for treasure—jewelry, ceramics, and fabrics desirable to collectors. As many as 5,000 tombs at Cahuachi have been looted. According to Orefici, "A page of history is lost every day which can never be reconstructed. But the place is so vast that our work is still useful in recovering at least some information, and we hope to be able to continue working in this way recovering pages and pages of the history of Nasca."[19]

There is proof at the site of a devastating flood and a large earthquake between AD 300 and 350, which led to the demise of the Nazca culture. Orefici's team has discovered dead bodies buried beneath fallen walls, and temples split in two. Apparently, before the Nazca left their destroyed city, they covered everything with clay and gravel. Perhaps, since Cahuachi was entirely ceremonial, religious, and ritualistic, they were attempting to deconsecrate their most sacred site.

Eden of the Andes

High in the Andes, at an elevation of 13,000 feet (3,962m) lies the altiplano, the high plains of southeastern Peru and northwestern Bolivia. In the midst of the altiplano is Lake Titicaca, the highest navigable lake in the world, where, according to South American myth, mankind first appeared on earth. It is one of the most sacred sites in the Western Hemisphere, and natives from the surrounding area still perform religious ceremonies there. The lake's shores are ringed with the ruins of small shrines and temples dating back to 700 BC.

Lake Titicaca, at an elevation of 13,000 feet in the Andes, is considered sacred to the surrounding natives.

At the southern end of the lake lies Tiahuanaco (sometimes spelled Tiwanaku), capital of one of the great civilizations of South America. At its center is Akapana, once thought to be a hill, but recently revealed to be a seven-level T-shaped step pyramid,

probably built to honor the creator god, Viracocha. According to legend, a worldwide flood covered the earth centuries ago, followed by a time of absolute darkness and cold.

Rising from the depths of Lake Titicaca, Viracocha, described as a large, bearded, blue-eyed man with white skin, journeyed to an island in the lake (now called Isla del Sol, or Island of the Sun), where he commanded the sun, moon, and stars to rise. He fashioned men and women out of stones, brought them to life, and sent them to the four corners of the world. He then traveled across the continent, teaching, healing, and bringing civilization to people. When he reached the Pacific coast of Ecuador, he walked westward across the water, promising to return.

At its height, around the ninth century AD, Tiahuanaco was a vast, planned urban center, with palaces, residential compounds for craftspeople, temples, paved streets, and pyramids. The population of the city and the surrounding countryside may have topped 60,000. Little of the original city remains after centuries of erosion, looting, and earthquakes. Stone once used for structures was long ago removed for other buildings. Also, late in the nineteenth century, more stone was removed and crushed to be used in constructing a railroad. American archaeologist Hyatt Verrill described in 1929 the extent of the destruction of this important archaeological site:

> This ancient American city has been desecrated, looted, literally torn to bits. Choice portions of its magnificent sculpted stone work have been carried off by the natives and used to build their own miserable huts, and there is scarcely an Indian dwelling within miles of the ruins that does

not possess a doorstep, a lintel, or some portion of
its walls formed of fragments of Tiahuanaco. Even
the rough, narrow filthy streets of the villages are,
in places, roughly paved with pieces of carved or
worked stones filched from the ruins.[20]

Although roughly 90 percent of Tiahuanaco's stone has been removed, enough remains to give archaeologists an idea of its precision workmanship.

Akapana

The Akapana pyramid, sometimes called the sacred mountain of
Tiahuanaco, is much eroded, and looters have gutted its center,
forming a basin that collects and holds rainwater. The pyramid, 54
feet (17m) tall, 646 feet (197m) wide, and 843 feet (257m) long, was
built precisely in line with the cardinal directions, like the Great
Pyramid at Giza. Each of its 7 levels was constructed with beauti-
fully cut and precisely joined stone blocks. No mortar was used,
and the stonework is so precise, a razor blade cannot be inserted
between blocks. Much of the stonework of Tiahuanaco seems to
have been carved so that the stones, some weighing more than
100 tons (91t), are interlocking.

In the center of Akapana's flat summit lay a small, sunken
courtyard in the shape of a perfect cross, with a superimposed
square. Recent excavations of the courtyard and the interior of
the pyramid have revealed an intricate internal water-distribution
system of stone-walled channels. These channels collected water
from the upper courtyard and carried it through the structure to
each of the pyramid's terraces before releasing it to a subterranean
drainage system that led to the Tiwanaku River. Scientists believe

that Akapana was built as an artificial mountain. Channels helped simulate water running off a natural mountain—on the surface or through faults and cracks inside the mountain.

Recent Discoveries

Excavation at Tiahuanaco began in the mid-nineteenth century, but was not extensive until 1978. From then until 1990, University of Chicago anthropologist Alan Kolata and Bolivian archaeologist Oswaldo Rivera mapped and excavated the site. After a decade of work, Kolata and his 11-man team discovered a mass sacrificial burial at the base of Akapana. The bodies they discovered, mostly of young men and children, were placed face-down in graves around the pyramid's base. Many were headless. Animal bones were also found.

This burial is unique because these "victims" may not have been killed there. They may have died of natural causes and been buried elsewhere. Then, after time, their mummified bodies were brought to Akapana, their bones pulled apart, and the bodies carefully placed around the pyramid's base. Radiocarbon dating places the sacrifice at around AD 610.

Kolata and his team also uncovered a statue of a crouching human figure wearing a snarling puma face, holding a human head as a trophy. This statue was placed at an entrance of the temple, perhaps to commemorate the sacrifice. Kolata believes the burials may have been accompanied by a drunken ritual, with participants consuming large quantities of *chicha*, a beer still made from fermented corn. He bases this claim on the discovery of the skeleton of a young man lying atop a layer of broken pottery goblets 2 inches (5.1cm) deep.

Excavations continue at Tiahuanaco under the auspices of the

Department of Archaeology of Bolivia and the University of Pennsylvania. The American team's project, called PAPA, or *Proyecto Arqueológico Pumapunku-Akapana* (Pumapunku-Akapana Archaeological Project), excavates near Akapana and at another structure, the Pumapunku Temple. They also conduct ground penetrating radar surveys in the area. Members of the teams are optimistic that Tiahuanaco still holds answers to some longstanding mysteries.

CHAPTER 5

Pyramids of Asia

Egypt, Sudan, Mesoamerica, and South America share the majority of the world's pyramids. However, ancient pyramids and pyramid-like structures, such as ziggurats and tumuli, can also be found across Asia—from the deserts of the Middle East, through the bustling cities of India, to the jungles of Southeast Asia, and to the Pacific Ocean.

The ziggurats of Mesopotamia, in present-day Iraq and Iran, are incredibly old and in some cases barely recognizable as man-made structures. Others, like the steep pyramidal towers at the entrances of various Hindu temples in southern India, are still in use. In China, tumuli, man-made hill-shaped tombs, may hold many of the secrets of early Chinese dynasties, and off the coast of Japan, some believe they may have found the submerged remains of a giant stone pyramid.

Ziggurats of the Middle East

At roughly the same time stones were being laid in Egypt for the Great Pyramid, civilizations to the north and east, in and near the Tigris-Euphrates river valley, were building enormous ziggurats, massive, stepped, pyramidal structures topped with temples. Various cultures that rose and fell in this "cradle of civilization"—Sumerians, Akkadians, Babylonians, Assyrians, and Elamites—built these temple towers. The earliest ziggurat dates from the end of the third millennium BC and the latest from the sixth century BC.

Ziggurats were solid structures, filled with sun-baked mud bricks and surfaced with hard-fired bricks. Layers of interior bricks were sometimes separated by reed matting to provide stability. The facings were often glazed in different colors, each

The reconstructed base of the Great Ziggurat of Ur, seen here, was built around 2100 BC and dedicated to the Sumerian moon goddess Nanna.

possibly having religious significance. Of the 32 ziggurats discovered in this region, all had from 2 to 7 tiers, with a temple or shrine at the top. Access to the shrine was provided by a series of ramps or stairs on 1 side of the structure or by a spiral ramp from the base to the summit.

Like the early Egyptian step pyramids, Mesopotamian ziggurats probably evolved from simple platforms, built one atop another. Unlike Egyptian pyramids, these structures were not tombs. Instead, they were monuments to the gods of Mesopotamia, and they rose ever higher to get closer to the heavens. Ziggurats were not public places. To Mesopotamians, these were houses of the gods, and only priests were permitted on a ziggurat or in the rooms at its base. Priests attended to the gods and thus achieved great power in Mesopotamian society.

Two ziggurats, one each in Iran and Iraq, are the best-preserved examples of this type of structure. The massive Great Ziggurat of Ur, in southern Iraq, measures 190 feet (58m) by 130 feet (40m) at its base. No one knows exactly how tall it was when completed, or how many levels it once had. It was built around 2100 BC, dedicated to the Sumerian moon god Nanna. Each brick covering this giant structure was stamped with the name of the Sumerian king—Ur-Nammu. Access to its upper levels, which have not survived, was by three staircases converging at a portal that leads to the ziggurat's second level.

Probably the best-preserved ziggurat is in the Khuzestan province of western Iran. Known as Choqa Zanbil, this ancient structure was built around 1250 BC by Elamite king Untash-Napirisha. It was dedicated to the protector god, Inshushinak. Archaeologists believe this ziggurat once reached a height of 174 feet (53m). They

Did You Know?

Ziggurats were solid structures, filled with sun-baked mud bricks and surfaced with hard-fired bricks.

have found massive reed ropes running through its core, apparently to provide reinforcement. Originally faced with bricks glazed with a blue and green metallic sheen, scientists feel Choqa Zanbil may have shimmered in the desert sun, much like the blue-tiled Iranian mosques do today.

The Great White Pyramid of China

Far to the east, in China, another pyramid shimmering in the sun caught the modern world's attention at the close of World War II. Few people link pyramids with China, and yet north-central China has more than 100 pyramid-shaped burial mounds. Each man-made hill, called a tumulus, covers an emperor's tomb from the Western Han dynasty (206 BC to AD 220). Because of China's relative isolation, few outside that region of China knew about the tumuli until the mid-twentieth century.

Prior to World War II (1939–1945), few Westerners had ventured into the interior of northern China, and air travel over the region was almost nonexistent. Then, on March 28, 1947, the *New York Times* published an article about Maurice Sheahan of Transworld Airlines, who claimed to have seen what he described as a large white pyramid while on a flight across China. Two days later, a somewhat blurry, black-and-white photograph appeared in the *Times*, showing the massive pyramid rising above flat, cultivated farmland.

The photograph had actually been taken in 1945 by a U.S. Air Force pilot, James Gaussman, during a military flight over the Shaanxi Province of China. Gaussman reported the sighting to his superiors, but the text of his report was not made public for decades. In his report, he described a gigantic, shimmering

Did You Know?

Unlike the Egyptian pyramids, ziggurats were not tombs. They were monuments to the gods.

white pyramid made of metal or stone. He claimed the top of the pyramid appeared jewel-like, possibly crystal. Further verification of the Great White Pyramid did not come until 1994, when German tour operator and author Hartwig Hausdorf visited the area, near present-day Xi'an, China, and returned with photographs of numerous pyramidal mounds, including the one seen by Sheahan and Gaussman.

The structure they saw was the Maoling Mausoleum, the burial site of Wu Di, fifth ruler of the Western Han dynasty, who reigned from 140 to 87 BC. His tumulus has a square base with 788-foot sides (240m), making it slightly larger than the Great Pyramid of Giza. However, it is much shorter, with a height of 153 feet (47m). The Maoling's sides are trapezoidal, and it has a flat top. It is unclear what Gaussman considered a crystal capstone.

According to burial requirements of the Western Han dynasty, construction of an emperor's tomb was to begin in the second year of his reign and consume one-third of the royal revenue. The tomb below the Maoling contains numerous chambers, each originally crammed with precious objects: full-size horse-drawn carriages; figures of tigers, leopards, and other animals; gold, silver, and jade jewelry; figurines; silk; grain; and other daily necessities. The mausoleum contains bed chambers, sitting halls, and temples for making sacrifices to gods or ancestors. Wu Di's reign was so long that, when he died in 87 BC, his tomb contained all the treasure it could possibly hold. Entrance to the tomb was gained through four passageways, each wide enough to allow a cart pulled by a six-horse team to pass through. When the tomb was sealed, sword and crossbow booby traps were set to discourage thieves and looters. Despite these precautions, looters vandalized the tomb.

Other Chinese Pyramids

In addition to the Maoling, numerous other earthen pyramids are scattered across this area of China. Some are flat-topped, but others rise to a point. The most famous of these is Mount Li, site of the underground tomb of China's first emperor, Qin Shi Huang. This tomb, archaeologists hope, has never been looted, due to the presence of poisonous mercury vapors within the tumulus. According to legend, the emperor ordered that he be buried in an immense underground palace with bronze walls, his body clothed in a gold and jade suit, resting in a coffin floating on a sea of mercury. All entrances to the tomb were reportedly sealed with molten copper.

Because mercury vapors have been detected in the soil of the tumulus, Chinese archaeologists are waiting for better excavation techniques to safeguard the find and the workers who enter it. Various noninvasive scans have verified the presence of a large structure under the tumulus, as well as a quantity of coins on the floor of the tomb. Archaeologists hope the tomb has remained sealed since Qin Shi Huang's burial in 210 BC. Numerous excavations near the tumulus have yielded amazing discoveries, including the famous terra-cotta army, found in 1974.

Additional pyramids lie in other regions of China. Recently, Chinese newspapers reported the discovery of possibly the oldest pyramids in China. One, in China's Inner Mongolia Autonomous Region, may be 5,000 years old. According to the report, 7 tombs and an altar were unearthed in 2001 at a site considered the best-preserved example of the Hongshan cultural period (4000–3000 BC). The latest discovery, announced in August 2006, is a group of pyramid-shaped tombs in northeastern China, in the Jilin Province, that may be 3,000 years old. One had a stone coffin that may have belonged to a tribal king of China's Bronze Age.

The Tower of Babel?

Scientists believe they may have found the remains of the Tower of Babel, mentioned in the book of Genesis, or at least the ziggurat in the ancient city of Babylon believed to have been the inspiration for the biblical story. Originally called Etemenanki, which means "The Foundation of Heaven and Earth" in ancient Sumerian, this temple tower was probably begun by Hammurabi, but its final stage, a nearly 50-foot hardened brick encasement (15m) was constructed by King Nebuchadnezzar. Today, little remains of the tower other than its foundation.

India's Gopuram and Baoli

Southwest of China, other pyramid-like structures are still in use. Hindu temples' entrances in southern India feature steep, stepped pyramid towers, called gopuram. The largest of these is at the Sri Ranganathaswamy Temple, in Srirangam, in far southern India. This gopuram, called Rajagopuram, or the Royal Temple Tower, rises from a base of approximately 32,500 square feet (3,019 sq. m) to a height of nearly 200 feet (70m). The ornate structure features 11 progressively smaller and intricately carved tiers leading to its summit.

The Sri Ranganathaswamy Temple is dedicated to the Hindu god Raganatha, a reclining form of Vishnu the Protector. The temple covers an area of 156 acres (63ha) and features 21 go-purams. It is the largest temple in India and the largest functioning Hindu temple in the world. No one knows its precise age, but some estimate it has been in use for at least 2,000 years.

Other ancient structures in India have pyramidal shapes, but not all pyramids rise above the ground. Where most pyramids can be seen, sometimes from miles away, India's baolis, or step wells, are inverted step pyramids. Chiefly near Delhi, the baolis were constructed centuries ago as water wells. First, a well was dug straight down, and then its side walls were gradually removed to form a descending pyramidal shape—sometimes covered with intricately carved stone-lined stairways that led from ground level to the water's level. The baoli that most looks like a regular step pyramid turned inside out is the Pushkarani, also known as the Stepped Bath, built in the fourteenth century in south-central India.

Angkor Wat

Angkor Wat, in northwestern Cambodia, was originally built as a Hindu temple complex dedicated to Vishnu in the twelfth century AD. It is part of the largest and best-preserved religious complex in the world. It sits atop a gigantic earthen stepped pyramid, called a temple mountain, representing Mount Meru, home of the Hindu gods. Angkor Wat is surrounded by a wide rectangular moat scientists have credited for holding back the encroaching jungle and protecting the site.

Angor Wat in northwestern Cambodia was originally a Hindu temple built in the twelfth century AD. It sits atop an earthen pyramid for protection.

Angkor Wat's central stone structure is about 5,100 feet (1,555m) long and 4,500 feet (1,372m) wide, making it the largest religious building in the world. It consists of three rectangular galleries rising to a central tower, with each level higher than the last. Each gallery has a gopuram at each of the cardinal points, and the two inner galleries each have towers at their corners. Each of these stone towers is topped with a stylized step pyramid.

The tower above the site's central shrine rises to a height of 213 feet (65m). The shrine itself was originally open on all four sides and contained a statue of Vishnu. The statue was removed and the sides of the shrine enclosed during the fourteenth or fifteenth century AD when Angkor Wat was converted into a Buddhist temple.

Indonesian Pyramids

Southeast of Cambodia, on the Indonesian island of Java, there is a Hindu temple known as Candi Sukuh that bears a striking resemblance to a Mayan pyramid. No one knows why the builders of this fifteenth-century structure chose that design. *Candi* is the Indonesian word for temple, and this one was apparently the site of fertility rites. Stone carvings on the walls of the pyramid and statues located nearby depict human sexual organs.

Also in Java is Borobudur, the ruins of a ninth-century AD Buddhist temple in the shape of a step pyramid. The structure is built of gray volcanic stone and comprises 6 truncated square tiers topped by 3 circular platforms. The peak features a central dome surrounded by 72 perforated stupas, each holding a statue of the Buddha. A stupa is a dome-shaped monument used to house Buddhist relics or statues. The walls of Borobudur contain 2,672 bas-relief carvings depicting the life and teachings of the Buddha. Devout Buddhists come to Borobudur on pilgrimages. Beginning at the base of the structure, they work their way to the top.

Some archaeologists believe this structure was built to resemble a giant lotus blossom, a central theme in many Buddhist myths. Evidence of an ancient lake bed has been found around the hill upon which Borobudur was built, suggesting it once appeared to be floating on the surface of the lake when seen from a distance.

Japan's Submerged Pyramid

On the relatively shallow seabed off Japan's Yonaguni Island, divers have found what they believe are man-made stone pyramidal structures. First discovered in 1995 by Japanese marine explorer Kihachirou Aratake, the formations resemble the sides and stairways of mammoth step pyramids. Evidence of dry-land plants and animals, and stalactites, which can only form above the water's surface, have been discovered at the site. If this stone structure is man-made, it would date from 3,000 to 10,000 years ago, when the area was a land bridge connecting the islands of Japan, Taiwan, and Ryukyu to mainland Asia during the last ice age. That would make them some of the oldest structures on earth.

Many geologists, however, disagree with Aratake and Misaki Kimura, a scientist from the University of Ryukyu, about the origin of these formations, believing them to be naturally occurring rather than man-made. No tools or artifacts of any kind have been discovered at the site, and similar stone formations are found nearby on land.

Many visitors to the area cannot imagine how such stonework—perfectly square corners, straight edges, and smooth surfaces—could be the result of natural forces. Some visitors to the area see this massive stone site as proof of the existence of Mu, a mythical lost civilization that supposedly sank beneath the Pacific Ocean as a result of some cataclysmic event. Others have adopted a wait-and-see attitude until specific evidence is discovered.

CHAPTER 6

Theories Old and New

Studying ancient cultures and their use of pyramids is like putting together a giant jigsaw puzzle that has thousands of tiny pieces. At times, a piece may seem perfect for a particular spot. It may have the right color and shape, but later, another piece turns out to be the right one. Some pieces are easier to place than others, but it still takes an exceptionally long time to reveal the entire picture. Sometimes, there are pieces missing, leaving gaps in the picture and making the puzzle's solution that much harder. This is how it is with pyramids.

Despite their location or age, pyramids are intriguing. And, because humans love mysteries and are obsessed with their solutions, many people through the ages have proposed theories about how ancient pyramids were built, why they were built, and who built them. New technology has brought new discoveries, proving some theories while disproving others. There is still much to learn.

Over the years, others have imagined that pyramids possess mystical properties and have formulated theories based more on speculation and supposition than on evidence. Still others, because of personal biases, believed everything about pyramids—their design, placement, and construction—was beyond the capabilities of ancient cultures and that native peoples must have been aided or inspired by people from other civilizations. In past centuries, this meant visitors from known civilizations far away, or from mythical lost continents such as Atlantis. Today, that list includes extraterrestrials. People with these far-out ideas, seeing gaps in the pyramid puzzle, try to force pieces to fit, whether they really do or not.

Far-Out Theories

Most of the time, odd ideas people have about pyramids are mildly interesting. Often, they are outrageously funny. At times, they can be frightening. In the mid-1800s, a once-respected French amateur archaeologist, Augustus Le Plongeon, published a far-fetched theory. He spent years excavating Mayan pyramids and temples. Somehow, he linked Mayan culture to the telegraph, the Masonic order, the use of the meter as a standard unit of measure, and the Jewish diaspora, the scattering of Jews in the sixth century BC. Author Sean McDaniel explains Le Plongeon's theory:

> Some 11,000 years ago . . . the sophisticated Maya "empire" created pyramids, temples, roads, and great art. Among the population were clever ocean navigators, the progenitors of contemporary Masons, and at least a few proto-Jews with long beards. Móo, eldest daughter of King Canchi and Queen Zoc . . . fled to Egypt by way of Atlantis. The

Egyptian people gave her a royal welcome—they called her "Isis" and "little sister"—and she provided them with pyramidal stone structures, paved roads, and writing.[21]

More recently, Dr. Delbert Blair of the Meta Center in Chicago told a 1998 audience that "pyramids were ground zero for landing space ships."[22] He also said they were built as communication devices by aliens in 11,000 BC. According to Blair, pyramids are strategically placed around the earth "as a vertex belt of

Experts and non-experts have many differing theories on how the pyramids were built and what purposes they served.

protective magnetic energy" to "balance the earth and stop it from being spun out into space."[23] Blair also claims alien-built pyramids under the Pacific Ocean are currently used by Northern Hemisphere telecommunications corporations to bounce signals off satellites.

On the eve of the millennium, one Internet doomsday report predicted that "former [U.S.] President George [H.W.] Bush and fellow members of a cult known as the Illuminati will summon oppressive evil forces at a black mass in a burial chamber deep inside the great Cheops [Khufu] pyramid. Even Satan himself might make a cameo appearance."[24] Giza officials carefully guarded the area, and to the surprise of very few people, except possibly those prophets of doom, the Great Pyramid remained silent as a tomb that night.

Currently on numerous Web sites, far-out theorists try to explain their ideas about the Great Pyramid and its place in the cosmos. Many have religious overtones. One, produced by the American Institute of Pyramidology (AIP), says the Great Pyramid is a divine revelation that lies in the center of gravity of the continents, in the exact center of the world's land area. They say it was built under the supervision of a prophet of God and that it is connected with biblical prophecy. They also claim it is mentioned specifically in the Bible, in Isaiah 19:19–20: "In that day there will be an altar to the Lord in the heart of Egypt, and a monument to the Lord at its border."[25]

Pyramid Power

Besides cosmic connections and religious significance, some believe pyramids, simply because of their shape, have special powers. One is American inventor Patrick Flanagan. In 1973, he published a book, *Pyramid Power*, that coined the phrase used by believers. In it, Flanagan claimed to have scientific proof of pyramids' mystical powers and an explanation of their "sacred geometry," the specific ratio of their height to the length of their sides.

According to the theory, placing food inside a pyramid preserves it from decay and enhances its nutritional value. This idea originated in the 1930s when Frenchman Antoine Bovis visited the Great Pyramid and noticed that a cat had apparently wandered into the pyramid's burial chamber and died, but did not decompose. According to the theory, razor blades and knives, when placed inside a pyramid, will remain sharp. A person sitting inside a pyramid (or beneath one that has been suspended overhead) will feel energized, with an increase in psychic abilities, and pets kept inside pyramid-shaped cages will become calmer. Cats may become vegetarians!

Claims made by pyramidologists, as believers in pyramid power are called, have been carefully tested and disproved, most recently by Adam Savage and Jamie Hyneman of the popular Discovery Channel TV show *Mythbusters.* Believers, however, remain unconvinced, insisting that attempts to "make it work" by testers failed, not because the theory is incorrect, but because testers made errors in their study.

Pyramid power has convinced people to spend huge sums of money to take advantage of these so-called mystical forces. One family in Illinois built a 17,000-square-foot (1,579 sq. m), 6-story pyramid home coated in 24-carat gold. In British Columbia, the Summerhill Pyramid Winery built a replica of the Great Pyramid and stores wine inside it, believing it improves the wine's taste. Salt Lake City's Summum Pyramid was built to match the Great Pyramid's orientation toward true north. It also serves as a winery but contains classrooms for meditation. A second pyramid was begun nearby in 2005 as a mausoleum to house the bodies of Summum's modern mummification process.

Early Theories

Mankind's fascination with pyramids goes back almost as far as the pyramids themselves. Egyptians from later dynasties were first to visit the tombs of their ancestors. They could read the hieroglyphic inscriptions and knew why the pyramids had been built and who built them. By the fourth century AD, virtually all knowledge of Egyptian hieroglyphs had been lost, shrouding pyramids in mystery. The same is true of pyramids in other parts of the world.

In Mesoamerica, the Aztecs, unable to decipher symbolic language on structures at Teotihuacán, theorized they had been built by the gods. By the time the Spanish arrived in Mexico, the Maya they encountered in the Yucatán knew nothing about the classic Mayan cities abandoned in nearby jungles. They could not read the hieroglyphs carved on them. Early settlers to the eastern United States, seeing mound sites like Cahokia, could not imagine that primitive native peoples constructed such monuments, so they assumed a more advanced people—members of the lost tribes of Israel, survivors from Atlantis, or descendants of Noah—had accomplished the feats, then vanished from the area.

In Egypt, the first serious interest came from Greek and Roman tourists, whose theories about the pyramids ranged from their being Joseph's granaries to secret libraries of ancient wisdom. Greek historian Herodotus wrote extensively about the pyramids and early Egyptian customs, but he could not read hieroglyphs and depended on secondary sources—priests and tour guides—for information. Unfortunately, they were not always accurate. When

Arabs first arrived in Egypt in AD 641, they knew little about pyramids but believed hieroglyphs contained mystical secrets of ancient wisdom. Not until the ninth century AD did they break into the Great Pyramid, because they heard a legend about a giant emerald supposedly inside.

Scientifically-based archaeological excavations began in Egypt in the early 1800s, but discovered tombs and recovered mummies and treasure did not answer many questions. The same is true of early civilizations in the Americas. The Aztec and Inca had been visited by Europeans, so specific knowledge about those cultures was more readily available. However, older civilizations remained mysteries.

Deciphering the Past

Accurate understanding of pyramids, both in Egypt and in Mesoamerica, did not begin until hieroglyphs were deciphered. In both cases, almost every pyramid and tomb contained hieroglyphs on interior and exterior walls that could have provided crucial information, had they been translated.

In Egypt, this process began quite by accident in 1799 as the result of a discovery made by one of Napoléon's soldiers during the French occupation of Egypt. Near Alexandria, in the Nile Delta, a granodiorite tablet, later called the Rosetta Stone, was discovered, with carvings that dated to 196 BC. The carvings turned out to be identical text in three languages—Egyptian hieroglyphs, Demotic (a later Egyptian language), and classical Greek. Initial translation was begun by Englishman Thomas Young, but Frenchman Jean François Champollion completed the work. Their accomplishment opened the door to truly understanding ancient Egypt and its pyramids.

The Rosetta Stone, seen here in the British Museum in London, is a granodiorite slab bearing an inscription that was the key to deciphering Egyptian hieroglyphis.

In Mesoamerica, much of Mayan writing was lost in the 1500s, when zealous Spanish priests burned thousands of manuscripts they feared were pagan and heretical. Unfortunately, those pieces to the Mayan puzzle were lost forever. A few survived and aided scholars in deciphering Mayan hieroglyphs.

Archaeologists began studying Mayan pyramids seriously in the mid-1800s, but specific knowledge of who, how, when, and why did not come to light until Mayan hieroglyphs were translated, a laborious process that began in the late 1800s and continued well into the twentieth century. Today, thanks to translators' efforts, dates of pyramid construction, reasons for building, and names of rulers who ordered monuments are available to scholars to give them a more complete picture of the Maya. With knowledge of the language, theories are much easier to prove.

What Can We Prove?

All scientists ask 3 questions when testing theories: What do we think? What do we know? What can we prove? These questions are particularly appropriate when studying pyramids. Within the past 10 years, several theories have been proposed about how the stones of the Great Pyramid were transported from ground level of the Giza Plateau to the upper reaches of the pyramid. Each sounds plausible, but further investigation will be required before these pieces of the puzzle find their niches. Until now, the most widely accepted theory for how 2.3 million stone blocks, weighing an average of 3 tons (2.7t), were put into place to build the Great Pyramid would require multiple teams of 25 to 35 men each dragging a stone up an inclined ramp. It would also require the placement of 426 blocks per day to complete the task during the 23-year reign of King Khufu.

In 1999, Americans Roumen V. Mladjov and Ian R. Mladjov published an alternative theory. They doubted that maintaining such a pace would have been possible. Instead, they believe workers, rather than dragging the blocks, may have rolled them into place. They initially based this idea on a simple hieroglyphic inscription found on some of those massive pyramid blocks—"This Side Up." Why, they wondered, would such a label be necessary if the stone was to be dragged up a long ramp and into place?

Remnants of large wooden rockers have been found in New Kingdom Egyptian tombs. Archaeologists believe they were simple levering machines used to raise stones into place. The Mladjovs believe that four such devices, lashed together around a large stone slab, would have formed solid wheels and would have made the block infinitely more portable. In a recent article, they explain how this would have worked:

> We envision small teams of men mounting consistently shaped blocks of two to three tons each on wheel-like devices, rolling them up ramps and sliding them correctly into place. The device itself would have been disassembled and brought back down from the

Did You Know?

Some researchers think that workers rolled, rather than dragged huge stones into place during construction of the Egyptian pyramids. They believe this, in part, due to the inscription "This side up" found on some of the stones.

California businesswoman Maureen Clemmons and a team of engineers from the California Institute of Technology proved a multiton stone block could be moved using the power of wind and a simple kite. Her team believes the Egyptians may have used this method in building the pyramids of Giza.

growing artificial mountain to be reused on the next stone destined for a place in the Great Pyramid.[26]

According to the Mladjovs, work crews could have been smaller and the stones could have been moved faster. Theirs is the only theory that makes any sense for "This Side Up" on the stones.

A second theory comes from California businesswoman and entrepreneur Maureen Clemmons. In 2001, she and a team of engineers from the California Institute of Technology proved a multiton stone block could be moved using the power of the wind and a simple kite. They used ropes, pulleys, the Mojave Desert winds, and a kite to raise a 4-ton concrete obelisk (3.6t) off the ground for a period of 45 seconds. Clemmons believes Egyptians could have done the same thing with stones at the Great Pyramid. Since Egyptians were able to harness the wind to sail up and down the Nile, she says, they certainly had the technology and the materials to have made this work.

Experts disagree with Clemmons, citing a total absence of physical and hieroglyphic evidence to support her claim. Evidence tells us kites were invented in China in 200 BC. Kites did not appear in the Middle East until centuries later, long after the construction of the pyramids. Finally, critics point out that her experiment used modern nylon rope, metal pulleys, and a nylon parafoil as a kite, none of which ancient Egyptians possessed.

Many feel that a third theory about pyramid construction techniques, presented in 2007 by Jean-Pierre Houdin, a French architect, shows promise as a missing piece of the Egyptian puzzle. His theory is a somewhat-modified combination of the two longstanding ramp theories. Using specially designed three-dimensional software to simulate the process, he believes lower levels were built using a large ramp but that internal ramps also spiraled upward from the pyramid's base, through which stones for upper levels were dragged. Evidence for such inner ramps exists at other Egyptian pyramids but so far such has not been confirmed at Giza. However, physical evidence at the site was sufficient to encourage Houdin and his team to ask Egypt's Supreme Council of Antiquities for permission to use noninvasive techniques to study the Great Pyramid. As promising as this new theory is, however, it is still just a theory, and some Egyptologists doubt its veracity.

New Discoveries Shed New Light

Across the globe, new archaeological discoveries, novel approaches in other fields of science, and the adaptation of cutting-edge technology for use in archaeology are providing a clearer picture of pyramid use in ancient civilizations. For example, recent discoveries in Mexico and Guatemala have answered some questions while posing others. The most perplexing for archaeologists involves a discovery that, although tantalizing and certainly of great importance in understanding an ancient culture, may never be fully explored.

Since 1833, crowds have gathered each Easter atop Cerro de la Estrella (Hill of the Star) in the eastern Mexico City neighborhood of Iztapalapa to reenact the Passion of Christ. As many as 1 million attend this annual event. In April 2006, however, Mexican archaeologists Miriam Advincula, Jesus Sanchez, and Maria Flores excavated the top of that hill and learned that it is not a hill at all, but a previously unknown pyramid from the Teotihuacán culture.

They uncovered stone steps and an altar, but because of the long-standing religious significance of the hill, the team

A Strange Pyramid

In eastern Europe, where no pyramids were thought to exist, Bosnian-born amateur archaeologist Semir Osmanagic claims he has found not only the largest, but also the oldest pyramid ever built. It lies in Bosnia, just northwest of Sarajevo, but to most observers, his "pyramids" (he claims there are five in the area) look like oddly shaped mountains surrounding the village of Visoko. He is convinced they are man-made, and he has a crew of volunteers tunneling inside to find proof. So far, they have found no artifacts that can be radiocarbon dated, only stone formations Osmanagic believes are giant, man-made steps. Geologists argue that these are naturally occurring formations.

Osmanagic claims the pyramids are 12,500 years old. Experts again disagree, saying the only people in the Balkans at that time were Stone Age people who never built a house, much less a monument of such proportions. Mainstream archaeologists scoff at Osmanagic, calling him a kook, but they are concerned that his excavations are causing real damage to medieval archaeological sites in the area.

reburied the site to protect it. Mexican authorities will have to decide how best to proceed, but some doubt they will want to disturb the long-standing Easter tradition. If excavation of the site is allowed, however, knowledge from the discovery could provide missing pieces to the puzzle of the Teotihuacán culture.

At about the same time as the Iztapalapa discovery, another was made in Mexico City. At the excavation site of Templo Mayor, Tenochtitlán's main pyramid, archaeologists uncovered an Aztec altar and an 11-foot stone monolith (3.4m). The altar depicts an angry rain god, Tlaloc. Scientists believe this discovery may point the way to a previously undiscovered underground chamber.

Finally, since 2002, a team of archaeologists have been digging at a Mayan site known as Waká, in the Petén region of Guatemala. This site, west of Tikal, features 672 monumental structures, originally thought to have been a relatively unimportant Mayan community. A recent discovery by Canadian archaeologist David Lee of the tomb of a female Mayan ruler, dated between AD 650 and 750, has led to a reevaluation of Waká's importance. Her tomb contained 2,400 artifacts, including stingray spines that were known to have been used in a male sacrificial ritual and a war helmet, both previously found only in tombs of male Mayan rulers.

Looking to the Sky for Answers

Scientists are looking more and more to the sky to help them solve puzzles on the ground. Infrared satellite imagery helps archaeologists locate new ceremonial sites, including previously unknown pyramids in the jungles of Central America. Mexican physicist Arturo Menchaca-Rocha is using muon detectors beneath the Pyramid of the Sun at Teotihuacán, looking for hidden chambers within the pyramid. Muons are cosmic particles that constantly bombard the earth. Sensors beneath solid objects, by measuring differences in the number of muons that penetrate, can reveal hollow spaces within the object. In the 1960s, a similar sensor was placed under the Great Pyramid, but no hidden chambers were detected.

Scientists also look to weather to explain aspects of ancient civilizations, hoping to help solve such questions as why both the Mayan and pre-Incan civilizations in Peru suddenly stopped building pyramids and abandoned their cities. A relatively new branch of science, paleoclimatology—the study of ancient climates and how climatic change affected ancient peoples—compiles ecological evidence that may reveal what happened to these cultures. This field also explains some of the social and political trends in ancient Egypt.

Brian Fagan, professor emeritus of anthropology at the University of California–Santa Barbara, explains how sudden climate change, such as a drought, flood, or hurricane, can have drastic effects on a civilization:

> Such was the case in Old Kingdom Egypt in about 2180 BC, when a severe drought that almost dried up the Nile undermined the ancient doctrine of pharaonic infallibility [pharaohs always being right] and the state fell apart. Earthquakes and El Niño devastated the Moche state of coastal Peru during the mid-sixth century AD. At the time, powerful warrior-priests with a rigid ideology ruled the state. Within a generation, I suspect that we'll have methods to decipher the ways in which Moche's rulers coped with the disaster.[27]

As technology is adapted for use by archaeologists, more discoveries will inevitably be made. Some experts estimate there will be more discoveries in the next 50 years than there have been in the past 150. In addition to increasing the world's knowledge of the physical aspects of pyramids, perhaps science will be able to assess some of the more extreme theories about pyramids and their powers and either prove them to be true or lay them to rest for all time.

Pyramids are everywhere, all around the globe. How they were made and who made them are questions archaeologists try to answer, and gradually, those pieces of the puzzle are being found. But one question—one giant puzzle piece—remains hidden. How could societies, separated by vast distances and having no discernible contact with each other, create such similar structures?

The answer, perhaps, lies in the very nature of a pyramid. Most ancient peoples believed their gods lived in the heavens above them. To better reach those gods, and to make it easier for them to see sacrifices made in their honor, priests had to rise above the masses. Temples also needed to be impressive structures, lasting for generations, and they clearly needed to demonstrate a culture's power. Pyramids fit that description.

We may never be able to assemble the complete picture of the world's pyramids, but scientists find new puzzle pieces every day. Babylonians built ziggurats to help them reach the heavens. Egyptians built pyramids as tombs for their pharaohs, so their *akh* could join the gods. Mesoamericans built pyramids so the gods could witness their blood sacrifices. All were reaching toward the sky for answers, and modern science continues that quest.

NOTES

Introduction

1. Quoted in The Editors of Time-Life Books, *The Magnificent Maya*. Alexandria, VA: Time-Life, 1993, p. 81.
2. Quoted in The Editors of Time-Life Books, *The Magnificent Maya*, p. 87.
3. Quoted in The Editors of Time-Life Books, *The Magnificent Maya*, p. 88.

Chapter 1: The Pyramids of Giza

4. Robert L. Breeden, ed., *Mysteries of the Ancient World*. Washington, DC: National Geographic Society, 1979, p. 57.
5. Quoted in Breeden, *Mysteries of the Ancient World*, p. 56.
6. Daniel Loxton, "Pyramid Power," *Skeptic Magazine*, June 22, 2005.
7. Quoted in Breeden, *Mysteries of the Ancient World*, p. 56.
8. Quoted in Breeden, *Mysteries of the Ancient World*, p. 71.

Chapter 2: Houses of Eternity

9. The Editors of Time-Life Books, *Egypt: Land of the Pharaohs*. Alexandria, VA: Time-Life, 1992, p. 20.
10. Quoted in The Editors of Time-Life Books, *Egypt*, p. 21.
11. Quoted in Breeden, *Mysteries of the Ancient World*, p. 70.

Chapter 3: Pyramids of Mesoamerica

12. Jorge Pérez de Lara, "Temple of the Sun: Celebrating 100 Years of Excavation at Mexico's Teotihuacan," *Archaeology,* November/December 2005, p. 40.
13. A.R. Williams, "Pyramid of Death," *National Geographic*, October 2006, p. 148.
14. Carol Kaufmann, "Sistine Chapel of the Early Maya," *National Geographic*, December 2003, p. 77.
15. William Saturno, "The Dawn of Maya Gods and Kings," *National Geographic*, January 2006, p. 73.
16. Quoted in The Editors of Time-Life Books, *Aztecs: Reign of Blood & Splendor*. Alexandria, VA: Time-Life, 1992, p. 28.

Chapter 4: Pyramids of South America

17. Roger Atwood, "A Monumental Feud: Peru's Caral is the Oldest City in the Western Hemisphere—and the Focus of Archaeology's Most Contentious Fight," *Archaeology*, July/August 2005, p. 19.
18. Quoted in "Cahuachi Peru," Ladatco Tours. www.ladatco.com.
19. Quoted in "The Lost City of Nasca," BBC. www.bbc.co.uk.
20. Hyatt Verrill, "The Oldest City in the New World," *Travel*, September 1929, pp. 12–16. Quoted in "Dating of Tiwanaku (Tiahuanaco) Site, Bolivia," Paul V. Heinrich. www.intersurf.com.

Chapter 6: Theories Old and New

21. Sean McDaniel, "The Lure of Móo: A

Victorian Archeologist's Obsession with a Fictitious Maya Queen," *Archeology*, January/February 2007, p. 50.

22. Quoted in *Michigan Citizen*, "Pyramid Power," September 12, 1998. www.highbeam.com.

23. *Michigan Citizen*, "Pyramid Power." www.highbeam.com.

24. Mona Eltahaway, "Egyptian Boogie Nights: Controversy over a New Year's Eve Concert Planned to Take Place near the Pyramids of Giza," *U.S. News & World Report*, December 27, 1999. www.usnews.com.

25. NIV Archaeological Study Bible (New International Version). Grand Rapids, MI: Zondervan, 2005, p. 1,090.

26. Roumen V. Mladjov and Ian R. Mladjov, "This Side Up: A Theory of Rolling Stones May Solve the Puzzle of the Great Pyramid," *Discovering Archaeology*, May/June 1999, p. 93.

27. Brian Fagan, "Archaeology: The Next 50 Years," *Archaeology*, September/October 2006, p. 23.

FOR FURTHER RESEARCH

Books

Brian M. Fagan, ed., *The Seventy Great Mysteries of the Ancient World*. New York: Thames and Hudson, 2001. Lavishly illustrated with color photographs, charts, and graphs, this book provides an overview of mysteries associated with many ancient civilizations, including the Egyptian, Mesopotamian, Mayan, and Olmec.

George Hart, *Ancient Egypt*. New York: DK, 2004. Lavishly illustrated guide to the Egyptian culture, including information and illustrations about pyramids, mummies, and religious beliefs.

Kevin Jackson and Jonathan Stamp, *Building the Great Pyramid*. Richmond Hill, ON: Firefly, 2003. The companion book to the BBC/Discovery Channel special. Uses the latest technology to support the authors' theories of the pyramid builder construction methods. Presents both fact and theory.

David Macaulay, *Pyramid*. Boston: Houghton Mifflin, 1982. Detailed, intricate black-and-white drawings and informative text take readers through the step-by-step process of building an Egyptian pyramid.

Elizabeth Mann, *The Great Pyramid: The Story of the Farmers, the God-King and the Most Astounding Structure Ever Built*. New York: Mikaya, 2006. From an award-winning series, this book tells the story of the Great Pyramid, focusing on the human element, the workers who built it.

James Putnam, *Pyramid*. New York: DK, 2004. Lavishly illustrated and informative. Hundreds of color photographs of pyramids around the world.

Web Sites

Archaeology for Kids Online (www.bing hamton.edu/cap/kidindex.html). Produced by the Public Archaeology Facility at Binghamton University in Vestal, New York, this Web site has links to sites about Egypt, the Maya, and other archaeological digs. Also links with information about archaeology in general.

Caral Supe Peru: The Oldest Civilization of America (www.caralperu.gob.pe/principal_ ing.htm). Official Web site for the archaeological project excavating at Caral. Produced by the Special Project Arqueológico Caral Supe, Lima, Peru.

Color Me Egypt: Egypt for Kids (www. touregypt.net/kids/pyramidsforkids.htm). Produced by InterCity Oz, with a store and links to tour companies, this site contains color pictures of Egyptian pyramids, maps, and links to other pages, including some that discuss far-out theories about the pyramids.

Dig: The Archaeology Magazine for Kids (www.digonsite.com/). This is an online version of the children's magazine, with special features such as Ask Dr. Dig, Test Your Archaeological IQ, an extensive glossary of archaeological terms, and kid-submitted art related to archaeology.

Egypt: Secrets of an Ancient World, National Geographic (www.nationalgeographic. com/pyramids/pyramids.html). This interactive Web site has information about eight different Egyptian pyramids, from the Step Pyramid of Djoser, through the Bent Pyramid and the Great Pyramid, all the way to the last Egyptian pyramid, built for Pepi II, as well as a detailed timeline.

Khufu Revealed (http://khufu.3ds.com/in troduction/). This incredible Web site, produced by French-based Dessault Systemes, graphically illustrates Jean-Pierre Houdin's radical new theory about how the Great Pyramid may have been constructed. Remarkable three-dimensional animation, beautiful music, and full interactivity. Requires download.

MayanKids (www.mayankids.com/mkintro. htm). This Web site presents a colorful look at the Maya—the people, their pyramids, their cities, and more. Also features a time line and maps.

Pyramids: The Inside Story, PBS (www. pbs.org/wgbh/nova/pyramid/). A NOVA Online Adventure, produced by WGBH/PBS Online, this interactive Web site features an awesome virtual tour of the Giza pyramids and the Sphinx, inside and out. Also has information about current excavations, hieroglyphs, and much more. A fascinating site.

Index

A

Advincula, Miriam, 92
afterlife, Egyptian beliefs on, 24–25
Akapana pyramid (Peru), 66, 67–68
Alecio, Mónica Pellecer, 50
Alva, Walter, 60
American Institute of Pyramidology, 84
Angkor Wat (Cambodia), 77–79, 78 (illustration)
Aratake, Kihachirou, 80
astrology, association of pyramids with, 17
Atwood, Roger, 56
Aztecs, 40, 50–53

B

Bent Pyramid (Egypt), 29–30, 30 (illustration)
Blair, Delbert, 83
The Book of the Dead, 28, 35
Borobudur (Java), 79
Bosnia, possible pyramids in, 93
Bovis, Antoine, 84
burial texts, 34–35

C

Cahokia (Mississippian city), 48–49
Cahuachi (Peru), 63–64
Candi Sukuh (Java), 79
Caral pyramids, 55–59, 55 (illustration), 58 (illustration)
Castro, Rubén Cabrera, 43
Champollion, Jean François, 87
Chicomoztoc (Seven Caves), 42–43
China, pyramids of, 73–75
Choqa Zanbil (Iran), 72–73
Clemmons, Maureen, 89–90
Clooney, John, 11
Cortés, Hernán, 50, 51, 53

D

Djoser (Egyptian pharaoh), 29

E

Egypt, ancient, 14–15 (map)
    burials in, 25–27
    climate change and decline of, 95
    religious beliefs of, 23–25
Etemenanki (Babylon), 76

F

Fagin, Brian, 95
Flanagan, Patrick, 84
Flores, Maria, 92

G

Gaussmann, James, 73–74
Giza, pyramids of, 9, 10 (illustration), 31
    age of, 12
    early tourists visiting, 18
    mysteries associated with, 9–11
    purpose of, 21–22
Goneim, Zakaria, 33, 36
Great Pyramid (Giza), 13 (illustration), 16 (illustration), 37
    astrological alignment of, 16–17
    construction of, 18–21, 88–90
    engineering of, 14–16
    theories about, 84
Great Pyramid of Cholula (Mexico), 53

ABOUT THE AUTHOR

Charles George is the author of dozens of children's and young adult nonfiction books on a wide variety of subjects—including books on various world religions, ancient civilizations, American Indians, the civil rights movement, and the Holocaust. He taught history, Spanish, and math for 16 years in Texas secondary schools before "retiring" to write full-time. Charles and Linda, his wife of 36 years, have together written close to 60 books. They live in a small town in west Texas.